AM I MISSING SOMETHING?

AM I MISSING SOMETHING?

Christianity through the eyes of a new believer

Ruth Roberts

Authentic

19 18 17 16 15 14 13   7 6 5 4 3 2 1

First published 2013 by Authentic Media Limited
52 Presley Way, Crownhill, Milton Keynes, MK8 0ES.
www.authenticmedia.co.uk

British Library Cataloguing in Publication Data
A catalogue record for this book is available from the British Library
ISBN 978-1-78078-026-9

Cover Design by David McNeill (Revo Creative).
Printed and bound by CPI Group (UK) Ltd., Croydon, CR0 4YY

For S, R, R and H.

Contents

Acknowledgements   ix

Introduction   xi

Part One: Minority Report   1

Part Two: Hopes and Fears   20

Part Three: Hold Tight   48

Part Four: Making Music   76

Part Five: Little Children   98

Part Six: The Lord Reigns   131

An Interview with the Author   165

Notes   175

Acknowledgements

Thank you to everyone at Authentic Media for their support and kindness; especially to Claire Ashurst and Becky Fawcett for their encouragement, wise counsel and prayers.

Thank you to editors Julia Evans and Sheila Jacobs for their great ideas, help and suggestions and to David McNeill for the wonderful cover design.

Thank you to Ruth Dickinson and John Buckeridge for commissioning the column in *Christianity* magazine, and for all the fun and support over the years.

I'd also like to thank the friends and family members who have inspired the various characters in this book. I feel so blessed to have such lovely people in my life.

And finally a special thank you to *all* the pastors and leaders who have been part of my church journey so far. Through you I've experienced the compassion and grace of Christ, and I am so grateful.

Introduction

Thirteen years ago, I'd have used the term 'evangelical Christian' as an insult. Now the label describes who I am. My journey to faith has been slow and sometimes bumpy, and I often reflect on how my attitude has changed over the years.

As a child I went to Sunday school, and I attended the junior school attached to church. I also went to a Christian youth group for a few years in my teens, but although I believed in God, I rejected what I saw as restrictive rules, and lived life accordingly.

I could also never accept the idea that non-believers and people of other faiths are eternally punished for not saying a 'prayer of acceptance' to Jesus. As I entered my twenties, I firmly dismissed Christianity.

At around the same time, I got a job as a reporter on a local news agency, covering courts, inquests and other stories for the regional and national press, TV and radio. And aged 24, I walked into the Wapping offices of *The News of the World* for a week's trial in the newsroom. Nine months later I was given a staff job, after a lot of hard work trying to prove myself as an investigative reporter.

Much has been written about what happened at *The News of the World* in the run-up to its demise in July 2011. By the time I left on 31 December 1999, *The News of the World* was already a deeply unpleasant place to work, and I was a deeply unhappy person.

It would be easy, however, to paint a totally dark and terrible picture of my time at the tabloid, but that wasn't the whole story. Life is seldom that simple, and the paper was often a force for good. And while some memories of my time there cause me to cringe with shame, I do also have some very happy and fond recollections.

I came into contact with many churchgoers while at *The News of the World* – mostly when covering stories of a minister or leader who had fallen from grace. I was often dealt with quite harshly (understandably!) by Christians who were hurt, confused and very defensive. Other experiences with well-meaning believers did nothing to alter my perception of Christians as judgemental hypocrites or woolly do-gooders.

But I still believed in God. As time passed, some of what I saw as a reporter began to wear away at the hard part of my soul. I started to become more distressed than perhaps a 'professional' should have been at some of the situations I was covering. It gnawed away at me. So I began to pray.

I prayed for the people I was interviewing; the patients whose lives had been wrecked by a surgeon who shouldn't have been working; a toddler who'd lost his hands and feet to meningitis; two little girls abducted by a paedophile on the south coast.

Then one day I stumbled into the back of a church, and prayed for myself.

Almost straight away I knew I'd been heard. I felt something subtle 'shift' in me and my life began to change. Six weeks after my 'cry for help' I left *The News of the World* after applying for a job I thought I had little chance of getting.

I started to drink less and tried to look after myself more. I started to volunteer as a press adviser for an international development charity. It wasn't easy, but my life started to feel cleaner, and I was becoming someone I could live with.

Occasionally I visited a lively evangelical church some friends went to, dipping in and out for a few years. Then two months after our wedding, my husband and I signed up for an Alpha course.

As I searched for God, I found Christians who showed me compassion and kindness. I started to understand the meaning of the word 'grace' and finally committed my future to Christ. But I soon realized this was just the start, and following Jesus was going to take me on a long, sometimes tricky, but ultimately exciting journey.

As I tried to settle into 'church life' I started to jot down notes and stories about my experiences. Writing helped me to make sense of what was going on. I soon found myself wondering if anyone would be interested in reading the story of a new believer coming to faith and navigating their way into church. The idea really wouldn't go away, so to deal with it once and for all I fired off an email to John Buckeridge, the senior editor of *Christianity* magazine.

I suggested I could write about my new-found faith; reactions I faced from Christians and non-Christians alike; attending a church that teaches homosexuality is a sin, while having close gay friends; learning to pray for people and coming across things such as words of knowledge. I received an encouraging reply, and a few months later met with John and Ruth Dickinson, who is now editor.

They commissioned a series of articles based on true events I'd experienced. The idea was to help Christians see how non-Christians sometimes view them, and better understand the issues that new disciples face as they go through the inevitable culture clash. I was to write under a pen name and change some other names and places, so I could be as honest as possible without upsetting people – and to respect the privacy of my friends and family.

The columns took shape with suggestions and support from John and Ruth, and as I wrote I found myself fascinated by the stark difference between the perception of the church from the outside and what I found as a new believer.

Sometimes it's been very hard to reconcile the two viewpoints. Now I'm on the 'inside', how can I relate to the people on the 'outside' – to my non-believing friends and family, my colleagues, the lady on the bench who looks sad?

Should I even be using terms like 'in' and 'out'? After all, wasn't Jesus much more concerned with those on the margins? I seemed to have lots of questions, but very little in the way of answers . . .

Still, I think the questions are important. How do we appear to unbelievers? Should we care? I came crashing through the culture barrier and lived to tell the tale, but what of those who don't, or can't? Are there unnecessary barriers that the church puts in the way of those who want to join it?

This book is based on the articles I wrote for *Christianity* magazine. It is not intended to be a critique of evangelical Christianity. I can truly say that when I walked through the doors of church for the first time as an adult, it felt like coming home.

I am, however, offering my honest thoughts and observations as a newcomer. I hope you enjoy them.

Ruth Roberts
Summer 2012

PART ONE:

MINORITY REPORT

Dear Dad,

I'm in church on Sunday morning, the sun is streaming through the window and I'm thinking about you. It's your birthday today and I'm smiling to myself because I feel like a little girl with some explaining to do.

You're probably surprised I'm here. The last time we talked about religion you said you believed in God but that Christianity wasn't for you.

Well, I think I've decided it might be 'for me'. Can I tell you about it? I think it's important.

Your loving daughter,
Ruth

* * * *

December 17th

It's Friday morning and my colleague Marie stops by my desk. 'You're going to hate me for this, but I'm going to church on Sunday,' she says.

I look up. 'Why would I hate you for that?'

'It's a carol service by candlelight and we're going because we thought it would be nice for William's first Christmas – and for us, of course.'

'Yes, and?' Am I missing something?

'Well . . . As you know, I haven't set foot in a church for years. So you'll think I'm a big fat hypocrite, just popping in because of the candles and nice carols . . .'

Gosh, these people must really think I've lost the plot. I shake my head, but before I can think of a reply, Vicki's talking, 'A Christian friend of my brother gave him a really hard time because he wanted to get his daughter christened but never went to church.'

And now Mark: 'My friend wanted to get married in a lovely country church, and the vicar laughed her out of the door, saying she only wanted her wedding there because it would look pretty.'

I don't get it. Do these kinds of Christians really exist? They're not like any I've met in my brief churchgoing career.

I have to remind myself that it wasn't that long ago that I viewed evangelical Christians as distinctly dodgy – and the people in this office know that.

But do most Christians really know how they're viewed by the world at large – however unfairly?

'Well, you wouldn't want to get married in my church,' I murmur. 'It's a converted warehouse.'

A few coughs and then an awkward silence. Great, now they just think I'm weird. And it's at times like this that I wonder if I actually have become a little strange. Surely Christians would want non-Christians to go into church for whatever reason, or am I missing something again?

I get a little frustrated sitting here sometimes. I want to explain myself but it increasingly feels like I'm speaking a different language.

I wish I was as confident in my faith as my friends Steve and Jane. They're so gentle and kind – just displaying the fruit of the Spirit, I guess – and people want to know more.

I know I have a long way to go to be anything like them, and my stuttering, incoherent response just now is unlikely to have led anyone anywhere near wanting to find out about Jesus.

But I do want to be a good example – I want to uphold Jesus' reputation, because for whatever reason, it's been damaged in this country, in the circles where I live and work. My cell group leader said last week that the Holy Spirit can work through any situation – often in spite of us. But I thought the whole point of being a Christian is that we're supposed to do Jesus' work for him.

My head's spinning. I need a coffee.

As I get up I see Katie, one of the producers, staring at me. And she follows me into the kitchen.

'I want to get married in a church,' she says. 'I don't go every Sunday, but I do believe in God and it is important to me. But my fiancé is divorced and I've just been told by the vicar's wife at my local church that there's no way the vicar would marry us. End of story.'

Oh Jesus, help, what do I say? Could the vicar's wife really have been that blunt, or has Katie just taken it the wrong way? Whatever the case, I silently vow to pray that she finds a vicar to marry her and a lovely church for her wedding day . . . and then the words, 'Tell her' seem to pop into my head. So I take a deep breath, and say I'll be praying for her to find a great church with a sympathetic vicar.

She mumbles, 'Oh, thank you,' and as she turns away I see a tear rolling down her face.

For the second time in ten minutes I'm speechless. Is God at work here? Through me, maybe, or in spite of me, more likely. I'm finding out that life as a Christian is often confusing, sometimes difficult – but certainly not dull.

* * * *

January 19th

'You hypocrite!' My friend Val practically spits the words out at me, and suddenly the restaurant we're in falls eerily silent.

I look down at my half-eaten pizza and sigh. I don't blame her for being angry. I'd just been talking about church, and she

4

wanted to know if my views on sex before marriage had changed. I've just told her that yes they had, kind of – me who lived with my husband for at least a year before our wedding day.

Maybe the clever thing would have been to fudge the issue. I do want to explain about my faith, though, and Val's one of my oldest and closest friends. But how come when I started talking about Jesus the conversation turned to sex and morality?

To be honest, I don't care what other people get up to. It's their business, not mine, and as far as I understand it, we're not supposed to judge.

But it seems I can't escape the issue. Just last week, my husband's uncle Dave was talking about how Christians shouldn't be soft on any kind of sin – that by staying silent we often condone it. Uncle Dave is actually a friend of my husband's family. He's lovely and kind, but does have some very strong views on what is the right and wrong thing to do.

I'll have to ask him what he thinks about the whole 'sex before marriage' thing. It didn't seem to be a problem when James and I started to go to church. Our pastor didn't bat an eyelid when we told him we were living together and planning a register office wedding.

That was one of the things we loved about the place – they accepted us just the way we were.

I look at Val . . . She's got me all wrong. It strikes me once again how big a gulf there is between the church I go to and the outside world. And it seems fine to be a Christian as long as it's a private thing, but once you mention the word 'evangelical' people expect you to start behaving all high and mighty.

Is that their problem – or mine?

I'm confused, and starting to feel slightly angry. Am I really required to start judging people who are living their lives in exactly the same way that I was until recently? I don't remember signing up to that.

I don't even know what I was trying to say to Val just now. No one at church has actually said to us, 'This is what you should believe; this is what Christians believe.' We seem to be soaking it up from somewhere, though. I know I'm supposed to change, but I'm not sure it's realistic to expect me to take on views and opinions that bear no relevance to my own experience and background.

How can I explain to Val about what my faith is really about? About prayer, how things just 'happen', and hardly ever in the way I'd expect or imagine? How do I get across what I feel during worship – she'd laugh her head off if I told her that sometimes I have actually imagined angels in the room.

This is the first time that we've come even close to falling out. And I suddenly feel quite lost.

I don't fit in anywhere any more. My non-Christian friends think I've gone slightly odd. But at church, too – I still feel like a duck out of water. They all seem so sure of what they believe and so close to God. I watch them raising their hands in worship and I know mine are going to stay firmly by my side.

I gaze out the window just in time to see a young woman taking a long, satisfying puff on her cigarette.

I've recently read of people coming to faith and being miraculously cured of their desire to smoke . . . well, that certainly hasn't happened to me.

People don't just give up smoking when they find God. That's totally bonkers, like healings and some of the other weird stuff I've experienced, like 'words' and 'pictures', and 'spiritual gifts'. Being with Val transports me back to the real world, where things like that just don't happen and evangelical church people are viewed as very strange indeed.

Suddenly Val's waving her hands, 'Hellooo . . . Please don't tell me you're praying for me – you've got a funny look on your face.'

I giggle. 'Actually, I'm just trying to resist chasing that woman down the street and nicking her cigarette.'

She smiles. 'Some things never change. Listen, Ruth, I'm just worried about you. What I don't understand is, why now? Yes, I can see that a few years ago things were a bit messy, but you got through that, you didn't fall apart, and look at you now – lovely husband, settled job. You're happy. You don't need religion.'

I sigh. 'Look I understand that this all looks weird to you, but part of this is that I believe God rescued me from that mess I was in, and so I want to say thank you to him. And I do think I need God's help to live my life. What I was trying to say earlier was actually about the mistakes I made. Had I known I was going to get together with James in the end, I would have lived my life very differently.' I pause. 'Does that make any sense to you at all?'

Val raises her hands in surrender. 'Well, yes, it does, up to a point, but surely that's what life is all about? You don't know how it's all going to turn out. You make mistakes, you fall down and pick yourself up. You learn. And you're a better person for it.'

I open my mouth. I want to say that I don't think I did pick myself up, that God did that, but Val's moved on.

'OK, fine. That's enough now,' she says. 'Quick, waiter, a glass of wine before she goes all happy-clappy on me.'

We laugh. And hostilities are over . . . for now.

* * * *

February 4th

I'm standing in church on Sunday morning and, if I'm honest, I still sometimes wonder what on earth I'm doing here.

Going to church is just normal behaviour for most of the people here, but it's not for me. Until fairly recently this morning would have meant a lie-in, reading the newspapers, shopping or tidying up the garden. Nothing subversive, just what most of the population of this country does. Church isn't even on their radar.

Not for the first time I think, 'How did I go from that – to this?'

I look around and spot some of the culprits almost immediately – the people on the Alpha course I attended. I smile when I think of what they had to put up with each week. Did they dread me turning up?

I had *so* many questions: Why did the Old Testament God wipe out so many people? What about the Chinese or South American people of 200 BC or before? Didn't God care about them? Why are Christians so convinced they are right and everyone else is wrong?

Now I think about it, none of those questions were really answered. The people, not the arguments finally won me over . . . and brought James back to church.

I turn and look at my husband and my mouth falls open in shock – what's he *doing*? James is standing there with his eyes closed and there's clearly something going on. This is a man who usually stands with his arms folded in a kind of 'I'm here in church but I'm a bloke and don't do emotion' kind of way.

To my horror I feel a prick of jealousy – firstly because he's having an experience that I'm definitely not having, and secondly because he's somewhere I'm not and is probably having a good time without me.

What kind of clingy control freak does that make me? The unease I've been feeling is now developing into full-blown panic. What's going on here? These people are all singing to someone called Jesus and I don't know him and I don't understand what he's done for me or what it all means . . .

I'm fighting back tears, but I manage to keep it together until the end of the song and the start of the ministry time. A pale young man takes the microphone and says, 'I think there's someone here who might be having a bit of a wobble. If that's you, then don't be frightened, come and join us up here for some prayer.'

My heart is in my throat. I've got to go up. I've never done this before and it's scary. I smile weakly at James and scuttle, head down, up to the front, imagining that the eyes of the congregation are boring into my back.

I'm feeling very vulnerable and hoping that I won't be left standing here on my own like a complete idiot. My friend Val's face pops into my head; I dread to think what she'd make of ministry time. Knowing her, she'd tell me I've joined some weird cult.

But I can't deny what's just happened. I *was* feeling very wobbly, just as the guy with the microphone said. How can I explain that and all the other 'coincidences' that happened before and after I became a Christian?

I look up and the woman who led the Alpha course is standing in front of me with a gentle smile on her face. I manage to stutter, 'Sometimes I just don't get it – any of it!' and burst into tears.

She spends some time with me and prays. Just before I leave she says, 'Some people make it very complicated, but actually it's very simple. When he died on the cross Jesus rescued you; he "saved" you, to use a Christian word. And now you are always with him and he's holding you by the right hand – read Psalm 73:23.'

As I return to my seat, James grins and puts his arm round me. And I think maybe I do know Jesus more than I realize. I see his kindness and compassion in the people here that follow him. I see his love in my husband's smile.

I don't know Jesus well, but I want to. The band starts to play the final worship song. And I sing with all my heart.

* * * *

February 22nd

'But it's pink!' I point at the soup bubbling away on the stove and the truth slowly dawns on me.

My husband has bought pink soup from the supermarket and is about to serve it up to our weekly cell group – *and* there are guests here tonight.

James looks hurt. 'It's beetroot and cabbage, and it was the only soup I could buy in large enough quantities. And actually it's rather nice.'

Of course, if I was a typical church woman this wouldn't have happened. Most of the females I've come across so far seem capable of effortlessly throwing together a nutritious soup and several varieties of delicious biscuits in five minutes flat, while juggling babies, husbands and successful home-based businesses.

I've never been near a soup tureen before in my life, and holding down a job is more than enough for me at the moment.

'Thanks. That's just great.' I storm out of the kitchen – just as two rather shocked-looking visitors are walking in.

It's the second time today I've lost it. The first time resulted in my colleague announcing, 'The Christian is swearing' in a *very* loud voice to the entire newsroom.

So much for witnessing to my friends at work. And now I've upset my husband and frightened the guests.

I go and find James to apologize. Then I notice that the soup seems to be going down rather well, so I start to relax and enjoy the rest of the evening.

Cell group is always great, but the end of the evening has always bothered me slightly.

After our worship time, the leader usually asks if anyone has any Bible verses they feel they should share, or 'words' or 'pictures', and sometimes I just feel freaked out. Is God really communicating directly to them? I thought that was supposed to happen rarely, not every week.

I've talked to Uncle Dave about this before and he says we are supposed to test everything – that's what Paul in the Bible tells us, at least. But he warns me not to close my mind to what may be happening – that words, pictures and prophecies are found all through Scripture.

If you'd put me in this room a couple of years ago, I'd have turned and run very quickly down the road. But it just keeps coming back to this – I know these people; they are kind, intelligent, lovely and funny, and I can't just write it all off. Because I know them, I'm pretty sure they're not making it all up – that something might actually be going on.

Sometimes I worry that years of interviewing all kinds of strange people from psychics to 'spiritual healers' has made me negative and cynical. But even as I'm thinking this, something is niggling away at the back of my mind . . . during worship, the phrase 'wading through treacle' kept popping into my head.

And now I feel like I'm back at school, wanting to put my hand up but worrying that I'm just about to make a big fool of myself.

I notice the cell group leader is looking at me. 'Anything you want to share with us, Ruth?' he asks.

I gulp. 'Well, yes, actually.' I notice a few people are looking surprised, including my husband, who nearly drops his cup.

'It's probably nothing, but the phrase "wading through treacle" is in my head and it won't go away. I'm not sure if it means anything to anyone else, but maybe God is trying to say that he's working in it. A situation that's difficult, I mean, not the treacle.' Oh dear . . .

Suddenly one of the guests speaks up. 'Tracy, what did I say to you as we were driving over here tonight?'

'You said you felt you were wading through treacle at the moment.'

On the way home I start to rant – at my husband? At God? I don't know. 'What is this, some kind of bizarre, cosmic mind-reading game? Meeting in someone's house and singing on a Wednesday night? 'Words' and 'pictures'? It's just not *normal*!

'I don't get it; it was just a fleeting thought. What if I'd ignored it? And why me – I'm hardly an example of godliness at the moment, am I?'

My husband takes a deep breath. 'That's all very well, sweetheart, but I think the point is that even you can't deny what just happened.'

And he's absolutely right.

* * * *

Saturday, 8.25 p.m.

Dear Dad,
Well, what do you think of that? It's not normal at all, really, is it? But I'm intrigued. I can't explain how I managed to 'pick up' on someone else's thoughts.

James is right; I experienced it personally so I know there is something in this. But I know not everyone believes that coincidences are meaningful; my friend Janet reckons they're just simple accidents, mathematical probabilities – and certainly not God trying to talk to us in a strange and puzzling way.

I don't have any explanations yet. I still feel like an outsider, watching from the sidelines. I'm fascinated by it all, and drawn to it too.

When I look at all this head on, though, I do wonder what I've got myself into.

Apparently, some years ago there was a mantra in Christian circles that went, 'What would Jesus do?' But in my mind what often plays out is 'What would Val say?' You know her. Fierce – as in a fiercely loyal friend – but she can be pretty scary too.

Last week she told me about a churchgoing girl at her work who was going to take her driving test the next day.

When Val asked if she felt ready, the girl rather piously said, 'God is in the driving seat' to which Val replied, 'Well, I hope he knows his Highway Code.'

I really don't know whether my friendship with her will survive, and that makes me so sad. She just doesn't get it, though, and I don't know how much longer we can keep going before one of us snaps.

Sunday, 7 p.m.

I guess the truth is that for most people in this country, church is irrelevant – and, to them, the people who go there are really a little bit odd.

I don't think I'm being unfair. It makes me laugh when I come across stories of Christians complaining their religion is not being given enough respect.

As far as I can see, the only time that church becomes relevant to most people these days is when pain enters their lives. A death in the family, or perhaps tragedy on a larger scale, a train crash, murder or bombing. Then the church opens its doors – and people flock in. They attend funerals, remembrance services, they light candles and hold vigils. And afterwards they seem to disappear back into their normal lives.

James and I went to church this morning, and on our way we stopped off at the supermarket to pick up some biscuits and cakes for after the service.

We drove down the main road, and on one side several football games were taking place in the park. On the other side there was a massive car boot sale. I mean, that's what people do on a Sunday morning these days.

At 10.15 a.m. the supermarket was absolutely heaving. I wondered what would have happened if I'd approached someone at the meat counter (or maybe the fish counter would have been more appropriate) and told them that Jesus died for their sins and would they like to come to church?

Perhaps they'd have said, 'It's not for me' in the same tone of voice you did all those years ago.

I'm still not sure whether it's 'for me' either. Being in church still doesn't always help. The worship music is lovely but when I sing stuff like 'Jesus, I love you' I don't mean it really, because I just don't understand. How can I relate to someone I can't even see?

It's not God I have a problem with – I think I've always believed in him – just Jesus. And that's pretty important when you call yourself a Christian, isn't it?

What's in my heart is more of a thank you than a love song. I can't honestly say I love Jesus – I don't know him that well – but I can thank him for putting people in my life that I do love. People who make me feel happy and secure – you, and Mum, and James. Or I can look out of the window at the sky, at flowers or birds and thank him for his amazing creation.

Can it start from there, do you think? Is that OK?

Tuesday, 3 p.m.

Someone at church bought me a new album of modern worship music and I play it when I go out for a run.

Some days I'm literally itching to get going and play these songs, push myself physically and breathe in the sea air. I think it's joy I'm feeling then.

But on other days everything is just too much. It's all I can do to drag myself outside. I'm hoping that the very act of turning on the music and playing it in my ear is enough because I don't know how any of the songs can possibly relate to me.

This morning I saw a man on the beach. He was in his sixties and looked as if he'd been a manual worker – a former docker, maybe, or perhaps a boat builder. Someone used to hard work, anyway.

He was with a little boy who was running around playing with a bucket and spade; surely his grandson, because on the man's face was an expression that moved me almost to tears. This tough-looking granddad was gazing at this little boy as if he was the most beautiful thing he had ever seen. He couldn't help looking at people passing by as if to say, 'Isn't he gorgeous?' I wondered what he would make of our church with its noise and its bustle and its emotion-packed worship sessions. How comfortable would he have felt with walking to the front of the meeting room for ministry, having hands laid on him, making himself vulnerable?

Maybe he'd be better off at another church, where he could sit on wooden pews and keep his emotions to himself and say thank you in his head to a God he never quite believed in, but ever since this little boy had come into his life he just wasn't sure any more . . .

I keep thinking about that man, and I'm struggling to imagine him in any church setting or context, and that worries me.

17

It worries me because if you talk to most Christians, they will tell you that if you are not a Christian you will not go to heaven. And I don't know if that's something I can ever believe.

But I don't want to think about that now.

Wednesday, 8 p.m.

Can I tell you why I started to go to church? I needed to. It's difficult to write this, but I needed help. And more help than you or anyone else could give me. It all started long before James and I got together and I felt very alone.

I did try to sort myself out. I also looked at other religions. But then I found myself sitting at the back of a church in Poland as dusk was falling on a winter's evening.

It was quite dark in there, and stuffy; candles were being lit and incense was heavy in the air.

I cried out to the Christian God, the evangelical God, the God of the youth group I used to go to. Whoever he was he heard me, and things started to change. Slowly, and in small, subtle ways at first . . . but they did start to change.

Instead of a sick feeling gnawing away at my stomach, I started to feel what I can only describe as hope, a sense of well-being. The Christian word would be peace, I guess.

But I had a big problem. As you know, I've always had a few issues about the kind of Christianity I was taught as a young person. And what I've learnt or seen since as an outsider scarcely improved the image.

I sneered at the kind of Christianity that says certain lifestyles are wrong. The kind of Christianity that seems constantly at war with itself; different factions, different views – everyone is right, everyone has studied the Bible and can back up their arguments . . . women leaders, homosexuality, spiritual gifts.

It was a battle for me to reconcile all that with what I found when I went to church one morning, some years after my cry for help.

I was captivated. Not just by the beautiful worship music that moved me to tears. And not just by the people I've met who have helped me to get beyond the image of a judgemental, petty God.

I'm pretty sure I encountered the real God and I do believe that, through Jesus, somehow he touched my life and rescued me. Now I just want more and more of him, and his presence.

I want the God who preaches good news to the poor, who comforts the broken-hearted, proclaims freedom for the captives and release from darkness for the prisoners.

This is the God I found at the church I go to. Can you even begin to understand?

> *Your loving daughter,*
> *Ruth*

PART TWO:

HOPES AND FEARS

March 1st

The solemn-looking teenage boy walks up to me and simply says, 'I'm thirsty.' Without thinking I hand over the two-litre bottle of water I'm holding, and he walks back to his friends.

I'm in South Africa with the television show I work for. We've been broadcasting at a school all morning, and I watch with a smile as the boy laughs and starts to share out the water with his classmates. There's no easy access to running water in this village.

Home suddenly seems a long way away. And the events of last Sunday are starting to shift clearly into perspective.

I should have known that at some point something less than wonderful was going to happen at church, but it was still a shock when it came.

'When you help out with other people's children, God will often give you one of your own,' the woman had told me. She seemed annoyed that I hadn't exactly jumped at her request to help in the crèche.

Fair enough – but she knows that we've been trying unsuccessfully for a baby for some time now.

Is that really how God works? On some kind of reward points system for good deeds? In my heart of hearts, I know that he doesn't. I can't help feeling manipulated by the church woman, and quite frankly I'm upset. I would help out more, but I often have to work on Sundays.

Actually, being here in South Africa has stopped me feeling too sorry for myself. Meeting people who have nothing but act as if they have everything is a humbling experience.

As I walk to my hire car, a group of ladies from the village smile and wave at me. They are each wearing a badge with a cross on it. One of the teachers had explained this means they attend the local evangelical church.

'It is a badge of honour for them. They are very proud that they belong,' he'd said.

I seem to be bumping into evangelical Christians a lot on this trip, and Olivia thinks it's no coincidence. She's my room-mate in the compound our team are staying in, and on the first night I noticed a Bible and prayer journal on her bed.

She's younger than me; she became a Christian when she was 19 and she is awesome. Her faith is so strong, and she seems to radiate it wherever she goes. It shows in her work and how she deals with people generally. Her enthusiasm for the Bible is infectious, and she was so excited when I told her I was a believer too. Every evening we've been sitting together just talking about God and church. I can ask her anything and she makes it all seem so easy – so *normal*.

We're up early on this trip, and at 4 a.m. this morning I sat outside our hut and read Psalm 40. I gazed up at the stars, listening to Olivia inside singing a worship song in her beautiful voice. Jesus seemed to be very close.

I think back to how my life used to be and how it is now. 'Bridget Jones gone wrong' would have been a good way to describe it. God knows I have some shameful memories that seem to jump up from nowhere every so often, making me wince. But God is giving me new memories to replace those old ones. He's giving me new experiences and new friendships. He's slowly changing my life and giving me things that I can be proud of – not in a boastful or self-important way, but so I can say, 'This is who I am *now*. This is who I'm meant to be.'

Is this what forgiveness means?

As I drive out of the school I glance back at the boy and his friends and think of the famous verse 'I was thirsty and you gave me something to drink' (Matt. 25:35).

Is it really that simple? I don't know. And there's an awful lot I still don't understand. But I know this – God is putting my feet on a rock, and he's giving me a new song to sing.

* * * *

March 18th

'So, can I still practice yoga now I'm a Christian?'

James's uncle, Dave, has come round to watch the football. The match starts soon and I'm shamelessly grilling him about church stuff.

'That depends on who you talk to,' he says. 'Why do you ask?'

'At work last week there was a story about a vicar who banned a yoga class from his church hall. I wondered what you thought.'

Uncle Dave smiles. 'Tell me more about it.' I sigh. One of the things I've noticed about Christians is that it's sometimes very difficult to get a straight answer from them.

'Well, I spoke to the vicar and he certainly thought he was right. I told him that I went to church, and he said then I'd understand absolutely that it's not biblical to condone any other religion, that Jesus is the only way to God. What I didn't tell him was that I'd actually just come from my lunchtime yoga class and the editor thought it would be amusing to give me the story.'

Uncle Dave frowns. 'So what happened?'

'Well, I organized a live broadcast. The reporter interviewed the yoga teacher while the ladies had an impromptu class behind her, in a different hall, of course, and the vicar stood outside and was interviewed directly by the presenters in the studio. The yoga ladies came across as entirely reasonable and the vicar looked like a miserable, out-of-date, stick-in-the-mud. I've heard Christians moan about getting a bad press, but I produced the item, and I'm a Christian. Well, at least I think I am. Sometimes I'm not so sure.'

James comes in with crisps and beers and sits down next to me. 'Did you try to find a Christian to give an alternative view?'

I'm getting cross now. 'Well, sometimes that's exactly the problem. The only people who will stick their necks out and take a "position" on things are the people who hold very strong views. And they seem to get all the attention.'

23

I look back at Uncle Dave. 'So what *do* you think?'

'I think you shouldn't worry about whether you're a Christian or not. I don't think there's any doubt the Lord has a very strong hand on your life.'

I laugh. 'You think so? The more I think about everything, the more confused I get.'

Uncle Dave takes a sip of beer. 'OK, let me tell you a story about you and James. A few years ago I was at a Christian conference, and there was a special call to pray for people who hadn't yet come to faith. You'd got together with James, but he'd stopped going to church some years before, and you both came into my mind, very strongly. So the idea was that we would write the names of the people we wanted to pray for on pieces of paper. So I did just that, and then we all took them to the front and put them in a big basket and we prayed. And then all the names were read out. Hundreds of them. And we carried on worshipping.'

Uncle Dave pauses, and for one awful moment I think he's going to cry. 'And that was it, until three weeks later James phoned and said you had started going to church together.'

That's amazing. I'm not surprised Uncle Dave's faith is so strong if stuff like that happens to him all the time.

But then something strikes me and I shake my head. 'But that's not right at all.'

'Ruth!' James looks really cross.

'I'm sorry, Uncle Dave, but it can't have happened like that. We didn't just wake up one morning, zapped by the Holy Spirit after your conference and think, "Hmm, shall we go to Church today?" We'd been thinking of going for ages. We kept meaning to. And I had actually been to that church before James and I got together; my friends went there and I used to go along sometimes and stand at the back. My point is that God was working in our lives way before your conference.'

James stops me. 'I don't think that's the point at all. We don't know how God works, and sometimes all of this is not easily digestible in a thirty-second soundbite.'

The football's just starting, and the men turn towards the television. 'I think that's why God sent Jesus,' Uncle Dave says. 'He's the person we're supposed to relate to, we can "grasp" him; he's the understandable bit in all this.'

I sigh once more, pick up my beer, and silently give in.

March 28th

As soon as I walk into the office I know something's wrong. The newsroom is normally buzzing with life, but today there's silence.

My colleague Sarah is sitting at her desk. She's trying to type, but it's obvious she's been crying.

I walk up. 'Are you OK?'

She looks at me.

'It's Pete. He hadn't shown up for his shifts for two days and wasn't answering calls, so Martin went to his home. No reply, so they had to break the door down and he . . . he was dead.'

Sarah starts to cry, and straight away my head is filled with images of Pete; Pete and I in the smoking room on the night shift, giggling away at some stupid joke that seemed hilarious at 4 in the morning . . . Pete banging his head on the table as he tried to be polite to a ranting listener complaining about our Christmas turkey item . . . Pete and I sitting together the morning after the London bombings and taking calls from frantic husbands, wives and parents who had phoned the TV station for help finding their missing loved ones . . . Pete talking softly to them, his face stricken.

Pete, who happened to be gay, who once confided that his very religious parents had never accepted his homosexuality and were ashamed of him.

Sarah is talking. 'We don't know the full story yet, but it seems that he'd just tried to reconcile with his parents and it didn't work out.'

No, *no*.

Now Mark, one of Pete's closest friends is walking towards us. 'It might not be what we think,' he says. 'But he'd tried to take his own life before, and had struggled for years with who he was. His poor parents.'

It suddenly strikes me how little I know the people I work with every day. Tears streaming down my face, I touch Mark on the shoulder. 'I'm so sorry. He was such a lovely man.'

'Thank you,' Mark replies, and we walk back to our desks.

Much later, I leave work and head for the train station. It's a chilly evening and slightly damp. I can't think about this now. I don't want to. And the very last thing I want to do is pray.

The church's view on homosexuality was one of the things that put me off Christianity for many years. Was I naïve to think I could just brush it under the carpet?

Bishops and archbishops can discuss the gay issue forever, but this is what happens with real people – they get hurt, they feel rejected and sometimes their hearts are broken.

Hate the sin but love the sinner. The words echo in my ears, spoken by someone I respect very much at church. How can it be that simple, when the 'sin' is who they are and whom they love?

Do I even believe it's a sin? As a Christian, do I have to? How do you know what to take literally and what not to in the Bible? In 1 Corinthians 14 Paul says it is disgraceful for a woman to speak in church, but women priests are accepted as the norm these days.

I'm reaching the station and starting to feel sick with confusion and grief. But suddenly I see her. She's sitting on the ground and she's sobbing.

I've seen her before. I don't know if she's homeless, but she has the pallor of a heroin-user. She's distressed, and people are just rushing past. I take a deep breath and crouch down. 'Can I get you a hot drink and we'll talk?'

I used to think that Christians were do-gooders, and I guess I've now become exactly that. But I can't walk past, and I realize that, for now, this is what Christianity means to me.

I can't make sense of what has happened to Pete and his family, and I don't know what to think about the gay issue, though at some point I know I'm going to have to work through it.

But in the meantime this is all I can do. This is all I have. I've made a commitment to God to stick with the church, to try to find Jesus and keep my eyes fixed on him. And that is what I'm going to do.

* * * *

27

April 14th

It's early Sunday morning and I'm pacing around our flat.

I've been putting myself through this every month recently. The pregnancy test only takes a few minutes, but the wait is agonizing.

James and I have been trying for a baby for a while now – long enough, it seems, for a group of women at church to start praying for us.

We bumped into one of these ladies at the conference we went to yesterday.

'We're going to pray this baby into existence!' she proclaimed, and I didn't quite know how to react. Am I praying hard enough for a child? Do I have the faith to believe that God will bless us in this way?

I was lost for words again during a break when a roving 'prophet' approached me with a quizzical look on her face. She explained she was part of a team whose task was to wander around the room and give prophetic 'words' to people while they were sipping their tea.

'And I think I've got one for you,' she announced. 'It's a bit strange, but I think the Lord is saying that there's joy in there somewhere. It's taking a while to bubble up to the surface, but it's there and it will come. Does that make any sense?'

None whatsoever. But I smiled serenely in what I hoped was a godly, encouraging way, and off she went.

Thinking about it now, I think she may have had a point. Compared to a lot of my fellow Christians I do seem to be suffering from a distinct lack of joy. It's not that I'm ungrateful – every day I thank God for changing my life – and I dread to think where I'd be without him; it's just that I still have a lot of questions, and a fair share of doubts. Why is it that when our pastor talked about the Israelites who were saved when the Angel of Death passed by, my mind immediately turned to the thousands of Egyptians who died? Didn't God care about them?

At yesterday's conference they were praying for people with serious and terminal conditions – and for people who've been told they can't have babies. I want to believe, but I can't help thinking of the despair if nothing happens. What if they don't get healed, God? What then?

Is it just because I'm a young, immature Christian that I find it hard to believe in all this?

A few years ago, the words 'miraculous healing' would have conjured up images of well-meaning but desperate people caught in mass hysteria, with a lot of scary shouting and falling over thrown in for good measure.

There was no hype at yesterday's event. It was calm, gentle and matter-of-fact, and I have no reason to doubt the people who took the microphone with encouraging stories to tell. But I can see with my own eyes that not everyone is healed, even though I read in the Bible that it's always God's will to heal them.

My three minutes is up now, and it's the moment of truth again. I almost can't bear to look. Sometimes I'm just afraid to believe, because disappointment hurts.

I read recently that fear and hope meet at the bottom of the cross, and that's where faith begins. And I think that's what's been happening in my life. Fear and hope are battling it out, and it's often far from joyful, but rather messy.

But I do have faith. Sometimes it's faint, but it's there . . . just like the pale blue line that's appeared on the small white stick I'm holding in my hand. It's faint, but it's there. Oh Lord, it's there!

As my mind processes what I'm seeing, a whole new set of worries fill my head. I walk into the kitchen and look out of the window. It's a lovely sunny day, not a cloud in the sky.

I've had enough of fear. What about hope? What if those people we prayed for yesterday *do* get healed? What if God does have a plan for my life, whatever the future holds? What if maybe, just maybe, everything is going to be OK?

I walk into our bedroom and gently rouse my sleeping husband. 'James, wake up – I've got something to tell you.'

* * * *

May 10th

I'm in the supermarket and almost walk straight into two young women as I round a corner.

One is crying. Her friend has a protective arm around her and looks rather cross.

'So you got drunk at Emma's leaving do,' she says. 'What's it got to do with her? I'll tell you – absolutely nothing whatsoever. She had no right to be talking about you like that. Honestly, you wonder if some of these Christians have ever read the Bible. All she does all day is gossip, bitch and make people feel small and then it's, "Oh, I'm off to church on Sunday." Unbelievable.'

My heart sinks. I want to apologize on behalf of Christians everywhere, but I don't know the full story, and quite frankly, I'm a coward when it comes to approaching people I don't know.

Some of my church friends tell exciting stories of laying hands on people in cinema queues or giving 'words' to strangers, but I'm not quite ready for that just yet.

I suddenly realize that I'm staring at the crying woman and her colleague. I smile weakly and shuffle past.

Sometimes I wonder why we spend hours devising new and exciting ways of drawing people into church when it can all be ruined by a thoughtless comment or bitchy remark.

I sigh and think of Neil. The colour literally drained out of my little brother's cheeks when I told him James and I had started going to church. He doesn't trust Christians one bit, and I don't blame him. He had a bad experience with some church-goers as a teenager, and he never really got over it.

Years later, Neil went to pick up his girlfriend from the theatre she worked in, and came across some angry-looking Christians protesting about the current show. Fair enough, but did they have to inform him that he was heading for eternal damnation?

And to cap it all, he then heard his Christian flatmate and friends discussing his lifestyle in far from flattering terms – when they thought he was out, of course.

I know that Christians are only too human, but how do people like my brother and the woman I've just seen get beyond these bad experiences and meet the real Christ?

My phone rings. It's Lauren from cell group. I tell her about the conversation I've just overheard, and I can hear the smile in her voice.

'Ruth, it's just people being people. I know you're concerned about Christianity's image problem and I know why, but God is much bigger than all this. And the people stuff works both ways. How did you get beyond your bad opinion of church?'

She has a point. It wasn't the Alpha course itself that led me to faith – it was the Christians I met through it. And it wasn't a clever conversion technique that first saw me stumbling into the back of church on a Sunday morning, it was my friends Steve and Jane.

They never judged me or frowned upon my lifestyle, and I don't think they actively tried to convert me. I was just curious about what they believed, and wanted to find out more.

Lauren carries on, 'Look, you have to trust that God will find a way to get through. Have you ever thought that in your brother's case that way might be you?'

Now, that's a very scary idea. I immediately think of the last time I saw Neil. I snapped at him over something trivial, and I could see he was really upset.

I can't do anything about that now, but I can do something about the women I've just seen. I quickly end the call with Lauren and head towards the tills.

Suddenly I don't care if I look a complete fool. This is important. I'm going to find them and say, 'I'm really sorry you're upset, but please give me a moment to tell you the other side of the story. The Christians I know are compassionate and they're kind. They're great company and don't judge or look down on people. You might find them with single mums or refugee families, trying their best to help.'

Now I'm a woman on a mission, frantically scouring the aisles for the tearful office worker and her feisty friend.

But they're nowhere to be seen.

* * * *

June 3rd

'It must be really difficult for you, working in the media. Every day you're walking into enemy territory. You should get some prayer.'

As I push open the door to the newsroom the words ring in my ears. Spoken by a lady at church yesterday, I'm sure they were well-intentioned. But yet again I'm left feeling slightly bemused.

Is this really hostile territory? It can certainly seem that way on a Monday morning, and when my boss prowls the office looking for someone to devour he does remind me of the biblical lion that Peter talks about.[1]

But I like working here. I like my colleagues; they are my friends, not my enemies. I know the media gets blamed for a whole host of evils, but I'm not sure it's that simple.

As I reach my seat I nod at Patricia, one of the broadcast journalists. Last week she let slip that she's been meeting up with

33

the parents of Pete, who died back in March. I asked her what they talked about, and she blushed and muttered that they just wanted to talk about him.

She's so kind and gentle. As far as I know, she doesn't have a faith. But surely Jesus would bless what she's doing, even if she's not doing it in his name?

As I log on, I wonder why everything that at first seems simple to me turns out to be so very complicated.

I know the Bible talks about spiritual warfare, and I think most of my colleagues here would agree that evil exists – they report on its consequences every day. But I can't accept that everything outside of the church world is controlled by the devil. There's too much that is good, lovely and heroic to explain away.

I glance up at my colleague Heather who sits opposite me. We've both been out of the office recently for various reasons, so I haven't seen her for a few weeks.

But something's wrong. It's nearly quarter to 11 and she's still at her desk.

'Isn't it time for your break?' I ask.

Each morning at 10.30 a.m., when the executives leave for their daily conference, Heather practically sprints out of the office, coffee in hand, for her morning cigarette. She's told me before it's been her routine for the past twenty years. But this morning she shakes her head.

'Actually, I've given up the fags.'

'Really? Just like that?' It's taken me ages to kick the habit, and there are days when I miss it terribly.

Heather sighs. 'You may appreciate this, Ruth, you may not – and it does sound a bit odd when I talk about it – but my brother had a heart attack three weeks ago, and I thought he was going to die.'

I start to say how sorry I am, but she holds up her hand and carries on.

'So I prayed and I told God that if he saved my brother I would give up the fags. And last week we were told that Jeff would recover. So that's it – no more cigarettes. I'm going to keep my part of the bargain. Oh, and I'm going to church now too.'

What? *Church?* Which church? Where?

I'm trying to think of what to say when Marie, who has been sitting quietly next to me, interrupts: 'I'm going to church too.' I nearly choke on my banana smoothie. This is all a bit too much, Lord. I've been praying for them both, but I didn't expect this.

I stare at the pair of them. Heather gives me a rather strange look but Marie goes on, 'Well, you know we took William to the carol service at Christmas, and it was lovely? Now we want to get him christened. Oh, and there's a very good school attached to the church and there's no harm in thinking ahead.'

I almost laugh. Church schools and bargains with God? Are they the best motives? I guess that's none of my business, but what do I do now? Suggest an Alpha course? Offer to pray?

As usual God is acting in ways I would never have predicted, and I wonder what the 'enemy territory' lady would make of it all.

One thing's for certain, he's in charge – and if this is a battle, then I'm on the winning side.

* * * *

July 15th

I'm in church on Sunday morning and something rather strange just happened. After always keeping a fairly sober check on myself during worship, I've just raised my hand in the air.

It wasn't up for long, though. After only a few seconds, I suddenly became very aware of what I was doing and started staring at my hand as if it didn't actually belong to me.

Then, feeling very self-conscious, I wondered how to get it back down again. Too quick a movement and I might take out the young woman standing next to me. Too slow and it might look a bit, well . . . weedy. I start to look around – what's the average time for arms to be airborne?

With my own hand safely by my side again, I wonder what on earth is going on.

Am I just following the crowd? Would I be doing this if I was attending a Roman Catholic Church or a staid Anglican establishment? Probably not. But does it matter?

It just seemed an appropriate and natural thing to do. I was thanking God for blessing me so much, for my husband, the baby that's growing inside me, for my family and friends.

The worship song is coming to an end now, and it's time for a break. My husband looks at me and grins. 'Well, that was interesting. I suppose now is not the time to remind you of everything you said when we first came to this church about how people worship here?'

He's just teasing me. And he's probably a little bit surprised. I think a lot of people who have known me for more than two minutes would have done a double-take this morning.

Val, for example. She's just about hanging on in there with me.

But this time she'd absolutely think I'd lost the plot and finally surrendered to religious mania.

I nervously peer over my shoulder in case a miracle has happened and she's actually wandered in off the streets, just in time to see my hand-raising debut.

Poor Val. She's still confused about what's going on in my life, and can't get beyond some of the more negative stereotypes of Christians.

Sometimes I just want to shout at her: 'It's not what you think. This feels like coming home, it feels safe. It's made a difference, and it's real!'

And I think I've worked out what's been going on this morning. This is real, and I want to take things further.

I'm fed up with watching what's going on from the sidelines. I want to get stuck in, give something back and really throw myself into this stuff. If that means I look like an idiot to my non-Christian friends, then fine.

It's ministry time now, and the pastor has already called people up to the front of the church and is praying over them:

'Lord, we want more of you in our life. We want more of your presence, Lord.'

I shut my eyes and echo his words, praying from the bottom of my heart. And when I open them again, I'm staring directly at a woman waiting for ministry at the front.

No one has got round to praying for her yet. And she looks a little bit sad.

I've prayed for people before with others in our cell group, but I've never had the courage to pray for anyone on my own. I guess I've always been slightly intimidated. Most of the Christians I've come across seem to effortlessly compose long, beautiful, prayers that really get to the point. At best my prayers are what you'd call short and sweet. My main stumbling block is that a lot of the time I can't think of anything to say. I'm well aware that it's a big thing for some people to go to the front for ministry and I wouldn't want this woman to feel short-changed. But still no one is praying for her. Maybe this morning I'm the best she's going to get.

Lord, please don't let me stumble and stammer; please give me something meaningful to say to help this woman.

And, preparing to shock my husband for the second time this morning, I take a deep breath and walk up.

* * * *

August 22nd

'You'd better sit down, sweetheart.' The call from my husband came earlier in the day, but the news is still only starting to sink in.

James has been made redundant from his job – and I'm due to give birth in four months' time.

Now we're on our way to cell group and I'm trying to be positive.

I read recently about the attitude of two men to losing their jobs. One was troubled and feared for the future, but the other was grateful and excited about the opportunity of doing something new.

I know we're not going to starve. James has a good redundancy package, and I will have maternity pay.

But I hadn't planned on this – and it's not the material stuff that I'm worried about. It's James. I can see that he's hurt, really hurt. He can't understand that the firm he's been with for so long has done this to him, just when he's starting a family.

This is not really about a job or lack of it – it's about more than that.

We get to cell group and find a quiet place to talk. James looks pale and tired, and I ask him what's worrying him the most. He pauses, and his voice shakes as he replies, 'What happens if I haven't found a new job by the time the baby's born? Will I have to put "unemployed" as my occupation on the birth certificate?'

I look into his lovely, kind eyes and my heart cries out: 'Please Lord, please don't change him; don't take away his confidence in himself; don't take away his confidence in you.'

James has always been so positive and sure that everything will always work out well. He's never had any problem with faith, since he practically ran to the front at a Billy Graham convention all those years ago. Even when he stopped going to church for a fairly long time he told me he never doubted the gospel.

When I go a bit wobbly and start to question things too much he gently steers me back to safe ground again.

Now I can see the roles might well be reversed and, if I'm honest with myself, I'm scared.

Suddenly, though, James's mood seems to brighten. He turns to me and says, 'Actually I think this may have been partly my fault. About a month ago I was having a quiet time during my lunch break and I did say to God, "Where do you want me? If it's not here, then please let me know." And two days later the talk of redundancies started. As long as God's in this, then we'll be fine. We'll be OK.'

I hope so. But I've got a strange feeling there are testing times ahead for both of us, and I'm not sure I'm up for it.

I really want to be the kind of person who serenely accepts God's will and his plans, safe in the knowledge that he is going to provide. But there's a certain amount of worry – and a need to control things – that's so tightly bound up in my character that I'm not sure I'll ever be able to be so trusting.

And what do we do now? If God really is in all this, what's the next step? Do we just sit around praying and hope to recognize the 'right' job when it miraculously falls into our laps?

In the past, big life-decisions have always been made based on what we've felt has been right for us, but when you add God into the mix it's a whole new ball game.

I look up. James is now telling Ben, one of our cell group leaders, about his lunch break prayer for guidance.

Ben nods and replies, 'Well, maybe there's a certain amount of work that God wants to do in your lives; perhaps you're just about to go through a time of refinement.'

I cut in, 'OK, that's fair enough. But maybe I don't want to be refined – I'm more than happy as I am, thank you very much.'

For some reason Ben seems to think this very funny.

As we leave cell group, he grins at us and says, 'Well, now you're really living by faith!' and I don't know whether to nod wisely, or punch him on the nose.

* * * *

Wednesday, 1 p.m.

Dear Dad,

People at church have been talking to us a lot about faith since we heard that James had been made redundant. But what does it actually mean?

To Val, it's a form of fanaticism . . . that's what she finds so difficult. You just can't seem to go to church and then leave at the end of the service; you have to get involved.

You can't just have a belief, you have to do stuff; they want your time and your money.

To me, that's the point of faith. I've never wanted to be a lukewarm Christian.

But what will it mean in real life? How do Christians live out their faith in tricky situations, like losing your job? How is it all going to work?

Another thought has just struck me. Do we give part of the redundancy money to the church? You see, there's this thing called tithing; it's a big commitment but it's part of being a Christian. Well, that's what I've been told, anyway.

What do you think about that? I know Val would go potty. And it does go against the 'normal' way of living – we're taught to look after number one, or number one's little family unit at the very least.

Our pastor has said he could tell a person's priorities by looking at their bank statements – not that he goes around asking to see them, mind you – but it shows the importance we give to things, I guess.

How we spend our time and money is important if this is going to be more than just going to church on Sunday to be entertained, like going to the cinema. If it's going to make a real difference, that is.

That's what Val doesn't like. She'd much prefer it if it was just part of our lives. Not something that colours it completely. She feels very strongly about it. I wonder why?

Saturday, 4 p.m.

Val's not the only friend who thinks I've gone loopy since joining the church. But living by faith does seem to put you at odds with nearly everyone else around you.

And I'm still slightly uneasy about some of the stranger practices at our church, such as being 'prayed for'.

OK, so at this point it would be fair to wonder what all the fuss is about, going to the front of the church to be prayed for. I mean prayer is fine; most people don't have a problem with that.

I'd better explain, hadn't I? I know that you're going to find all of this odd. It's just that at the church I go to, praying for people means 'laying hands on them' and kind of praying into their ear.

You're supposed to place your hand on their shoulder or, if you're praying for healing, on the afflicted part of the body (within reason, of course). Then you look for signs that something called the Holy Spirit is at work. Possible signs include your face flushing, eyelids blinking even though your eyes are closed, and sometimes a slight swaying movement.

I still haven't worked out exactly what the Holy Spirit is, but I've been told it's something to do with the presence of God.

Sometimes people get so overcome by the Holy Spirit that they fall over or start to jump around and get very excited. I know, I know.

When I'm being prayed for, though, I feel very peaceful, if a little unnerved.

But it's still a very odd feeling to let someone who you don't know invade your personal space in this way. It's uncomfortable to know that you are being watched so closely . . . sometimes other people come and join in the praying too.

People also offer 'words' and 'pictures' to the person being prayed for. These are supposed to be helpful, encouraging, and from God to build people up. Supernatural of course, and so something else that would make Val think I'd lost the plot.

'Words' and 'pictures' can sometimes be a little bizarre. I'm still trying to get my head round the raspberry pavlova 'word' that James and I were 'given' shortly after we found out he'd lost his job.

A very earnest and sweet young woman at our cell group said she was getting a picture of a raspberry pavlova in her head. She announced, 'I think it could mean this. You are the raspberries, James is the cream, and Jesus is the meringue base. You're all in this together.'

And I don't think she was joking.

Sunday, 8 p.m.

Well I know what you're thinking now. Does having faith mean you have to leave your brain at the door of the church?

Last week I read about Christian groups in America who actually handle deadly snakes in their Sunday services because of a passage in the Bible that says 'They shall take up serpents . . .'[2] They would claim they were stepping out in faith and trusting God to protect them, but quite a few of them have been bitten and some have died. Well, there you go.

I guess it's easy for me to look at strange practices and think that's a million miles away from where I'm at. But there have been cases in this country of people dying after they stopped taking life-saving medicines, so sure were they that God would heal them.

That's another reason why I love the church I go to. They have what they call a 'holistic' approach. Our pastor stresses we should definitely pray for healing, but go to the doctor too – God can heal in many different ways, sometimes through faith as well as through the medical profession.

I'm not sure the snake-handling Christians would agree. Oh, I forgot to mention earlier that some of them have also been known to drink deadly poisons as a way of proving their faith. Head-spinning stuff. There's one thing I've found in the last few years – there's nothing simple about Christianity. There should be a course I could go on to help explain it all. What about 'Hearing from God: How to Recognize the Voice of the Almighty in Ten Easy Steps'. That would be nice, not to say helpful. Or maybe someone should devise a special guide to what different types of Christians believe – and why they believe it.

When you first come to faith, you could be asked to take some kind of a personality and opinions test which matches you with the kind of church most suited to you and your beliefs. 'There you are, charismatic Catholic – off you go! Evangelical Anglican – down the road and turn right at the traffic lights.' Knowing my luck at the moment I'd be matched to the strychnine-quaffing snake fans.

45

Tuesday, 8 p.m.

I'm still thinking about the snake handlers and wondering about exactly how faith works out in real life – especially when the going gets hard.

According to Mark's Gospel, Jesus talked about snakes and poison just before he ascended to heaven. He is quoted as saying, 'And these signs will accompany those who believe: In my name they will drive out demons; they will speak in new tongues; they will pick up snakes with their hands; and when they drink deadly poison, it will not hurt them at all; they will place their hands on sick people, and they will get well.' [3]

I guess the snake people would argue that you can't just ignore certain parts of the Bible just because they are inconvenient. Perhaps they are right.

Mind you, this does come from a passage of the Bible that is disputed, and not found in the earliest texts. Arghh, frustrating, isn't it?

It's been a few weeks now and James still hasn't found work. We've been trying to pray about it, but I do wonder if there is the 'perfect' job out there for him.

Is there some kind of a mystical Yellow Brick Road out there for us – all we have to do is look for the right signs, faithfully read our Bibles and pray, and God's right plan will unfold for our lives?

Our situation reminds me of Christian attitudes I've come across to moving house. Some people at our church pray really hard about that sort of thing. One woman I know thought

*God had 'told' her that she would be living in a house with a
white picket fence and she spent all her time looking for one
in estate agents' windows.*

*I don't know if I think it's normal to go hunting the neigh-
bourhood for white picket fences. Does God really want us to
have the perfect house – or job? Is he really interested in the
tiny details of our little lives?*

*And what happens if we get it wrong? What if we head off
the wrong way? Will we be able to get back again? Another
preacher I heard recently said God won't take you anywhere
without giving you the strength to cope. That's all very well
but I'd rather avoid the journey in the first place.*

Saturday, 10 p.m.

*I don't think I'm struggling at the moment – but the job thing
has put everything in sharp focus.*

*Writing to you, too, is obviously making me think. And I
think at the moment I'm more bemused than anything else.*

Trust me, living by faith is not easy.

I'd better get some sleep.

> *Your loving daughter,*
> *Ruth*

PART THREE:

HOLD TIGHT

October 3rd

I'm sitting round the table at cell group and I seem to be the only person not laughing.

Jack is telling a story of a Christian friend who recently came across a homeless person on his way home from work, 'So, he clearly felt God saying to him, "Go and punch that man in the stomach." Strange request, I know, but he's not one to ignore the Holy Spirit. So he did what he was told, and it turns out that the homeless guy had been suffering from stomach ulcers and he was healed right there on the spot! Amazing.'

Talking of stomachs, I feel sick right to the pit of mine. I really struggle with this kind of stuff. I struggled a few months ago when I saw footage of a preacher in Florida kneeing someone in the stomach and boasting about kicking an old lady – because God had told him to.

Back at the table the group is joking about how this new type of 'healing' could be very useful in settling scores with people you've had past issues with.

I'm not in the mood for this and, before I really think about it, I've opened my mouth.

'I'm sorry, but I don't think this is funny.' The room goes silent. 'I'm well aware that I'm going to be seen as a party-pooper, and maybe I have had a massive sense of humour failure, but I really don't get the joke.'

Some people are looking a bit shocked. I don't think they've seen this side of me before, possibly because I try to hide the stroppy, grumpy part – at church, anyway.

But actually sometimes I'm just fed up with trying to be nice and diplomatic. Is this what Christianity is all about? I feel like I've become a bit, well, *fluffy* recently. Why can't I occasionally speak my mind and not care about offending people?

'So you think Jesus is just meek and mild, Ruth, is that it?' Jack seems to read my thoughts, but he's talking about punching the homeless man again.

What's going on here? Why is going around physically assaulting people suddenly acceptable because it's being done in the name of God?

When this kind of stuff comes up I feel as if I've been catapulted into a bizarre world where people I know and love suddenly seem like strangers to me.

I see James trying to catch my eye; he's making a kind of 'calm down' motion with his hands but this only serves to enrage me more.

I start to rant. 'No, I don't think Jesus is meek and mild, but I don't remember reading in the Gospels about him kicking or punching people. How did your friend know that he had healed this guy? Did he take him to the hospital, get him scanned and wait days for the test results?'

The room has gone very quiet. People are looking upset. I hold my hands up.

'Look, I'm sorry, but I don't know how I'm going to get past this. It just scares me when people are so *sure* that they've heard from God. I'm new to all this, and if I'm praying for someone and I think I have a word or a picture for them and I get it wrong that's fine, but if I punch someone in the stomach and I've got it wrong – well, what then?'

I look around the room. Great. Now what have I done? These people have been so lovely. I remember how they cheered when we announced I was pregnant, and groaned when James was made redundant. Now I've offended them and it will never be the same again. Tears of self-pity are rolling down my cheeks but I don't know how to stop them.

It takes me a few seconds to realize what is happening, but one of the ladies I've become quite close to is giving me a hug. Others are smiling. They're not angry with me, and despite my ungracious strop just now, they are actually trying to make me feel better.

It strikes me again how strange it is to be thrown into a room full of people that you don't know at all. In most cases, the only thing we've got in common is church. We eat together and sing together, we 'share' really personal stuff, and sometimes we cry together. Some of the people around me really get on my nerves, and I'm sure tonight's not the first night I've managed to upset or offend.

I look around the room and see Monica, who's said on several occasions she would very much like to be married and have children, but feels she's running out of time. I wonder what it means for her to come to a group like this, with several young couples. What happens when she goes home after yet another new baby is joyously handed around the room?

Then there's Gideon, who has very strong views on the absolute authority of the Bible. He keeps giving me very strange looks, and I'm worried he's gearing himself up to ask why I haven't yet signed his petition supporting traditional marriage. I doubt he'd be easily deterred; it's rumoured he once kept up an online debate with a so-called 'liberal' vicar for a fortnight.

Over by the door I see 'Headline Phil', one of the few people on this planet who manages to rile my normally mild-mannered husband on a regular basis, usually by cornering him and demanding to know his 'headlines'.

And here we go, he's at it again. I try to get up as gracefully as I can for a woman 'with child', but it's too late.

'So James, how's your week been?'

'Oh, fine thanks, yes, we're doing OK.'

'No, come on, what's really happening, hmmm? Your *headlines*, yes?'

James has confided he fears one day he'll snap and say what's really going on. 'BONG: Still unemployed. BONG: Baby due in two months' time. BONG: If you ask me about my headlines again I won't be responsible for my actions . . .'

I start to giggle. Is there anything similar in our culture that cell group could be compared to? A choir? Book club? Group therapy session?

Not really. Because actually these people in this room have become like family to me. But in a gritty, we're with you, warts-and-all kind of way – there's nothing sentimental about it. We may not always agree with each other, but we'll stick together anyway.

And I think it's dawning on me that this is how God intended his church to be.

* * * *

November 25th

I'm just about to walk into church for the Sunday morning service, and I still can't quite believe that Neil is by my side.

My brother's very dim view of evangelical Christians hasn't changed in the past few months. As far as I'm aware he still thinks believers are obsessed with hell and damnation, and I really hope that subject doesn't come up today.

All things considered, it's a minor miracle he's here. Neil sometimes stays with my husband and me on Saturday nights, and then we all go for Sunday lunch – but church has never been on the agenda. Then last night he stumbled into our room, clearly the worse for wear after a night out with friends, and announced he was going to come to church.

'It's about time I saw what goes on in this place,' he said. 'Just to check up on you, mind. You're not going to *get* me, you're not – ha!'

I was fully expecting him to change his mind at breakfast, but here he is now, politely smiling at the greeters on the door.

Perhaps he's still a bit drunk and is not quite sure what he's doing.

'Well, they all look normal enough,' he says, nervously, as we find a seat, and I wonder how he's going to react when the service begins.

We're a fairly mixed bunch when it comes to worship – some people are happy just to sing enthusiastically, many raise their hands in the air, and others jump, shout, shake and fall to their knees.

I used to be enthralled when I first started coming, but now it just seems, well – normal to me.

Neil is not alone in being wary of lively churches. Most of my non-Christians friends say they've seen TV footage that puts them off, and they think it's all a bit too much.

I've tried to compare it with people chanting and singing at football matches or waving their hands in the air at music festivals, to no avail.

Obviously some visitors to church manage to get beyond the culture shock, but what happens if they don't? Should people tone down their reactions to the Holy Spirit in case they put newcomers off their stride?

Well, I'm certainly going to with my brother sitting next to me. There will be no hand waving for me this morning. Or am I just being a coward?

It all starts quite well. The band begins with a rousing version of 'Amazing Grace' and Neil looks moved, almost tearful. But during the second song, disaster strikes. The man in front of Neil starts to slowly jiggle, and then breaks out into a full-blown, out of step dance with lots of arm-waving thrown in for good measure.

I've seen this man before. He's actually a well-respected GP. I once sat behind him at a family service and giggled when his 8-year-old son tugged at his mother's arm and said, 'Oh no, Muuum! Dad's dancing again.'

But it's all too much for Neil. He looks horrified and upset. I watch as he stares around the room.

People are closing their eyes, raising their hands and generally becoming lost in worship to a God my brother doesn't know or understand.

Finally he says, 'I'm sorry,' and practically runs out of the room. He doesn't return.

Later I find him outside. He looks peaceful, sitting under a tree and puffing away on his cigarette. As I approach I almost feel as if I'm interrupting a prayer. Whatever's going on, I really hope his experience just now is not going to damage our relationship in any way. But to my relief he smiles at the sight of his heavily pregnant sister waddling along, and stubs out his cigarette.

'Mustn't let smoke get near the baby,' he grins, and we sit in silence for a while.

Finally he speaks. 'I'd just like you to know that I respect your beliefs, and if that kind of thing helps you and James, then great. But let's be clear about one thing. I am never going to set foot in this church ever again.'

54

Oh yes, he will. Because when this baby of ours makes an appearance I'm going to get him or her baptized, and Uncle Neil won't be able to stay away.

He's come this far. Who knows what's going to happen next?

* * * *

Tuesday, 4 p.m.

Dear Dad,
Well, here it is, the news I've been waiting to tell you: You're a granddad!

Daniel John arrived just after midday on Saturday, 7lbs and 5 ounces, and he's totally gorgeous.

I can't remember too much about the labour; it all happened quite quickly and in the end they used forceps to get him out. He didn't cry straight away. The midwife had him and it hit me hard. Sheer terror. I could only whisper, 'Is everything OK?'

He started crying then, screaming in fact, and we were presented with this red, wriggling creature. 'A little boy!' we said. 'Oh, hello! Hello, baby!'

I looked at James and he was crying too. And Daniel stopped yelling and frowned at us, totally bemused. I didn't blame him.

Now he doesn't want to be parted from me at all, and starts to cry every time I try to put him in his Moses basket.

At the hospital I watched the other babies lying happily in their cots. The midwife saw I was having trouble and swaddled him in a soft blanket, gently put him down and he went to sleep. Not for long, though. I'd studied the swaddling very carefully and tried to do exactly what the midwife had done, but it unravelled almost straight away.

I'm just not good with stuff like that. I can't even wrap a present neatly. When Val comes over, she goes around straightening everything in the flat – towels, tablecloths, the throw on the sofa. I'm sure she'd straighten my clothes if I'd let her.

You don't want to know the gory details, but I can't actually sit up at the moment and that's OK with me for now. I'm quite happy lying in bed with Daniel next to me. It's the only way we get any sleep.

James has been far too polite to mention the row we had after the antenatal class when I declared I absolutely would never have my baby in bed with me. But James is good like that. I've been so blessed to have him, Dad. And so blessed with this baby, this tiny, funny little being.

I think I was worried I'd be out of my depth; I mean, I don't know one end of a baby from the other. But I'm besotted. I'm happy just to watch him for hours. I think we're going to get along just fine.

Mum came to the hospital straight from the station to meet her first grandchild. Neil arrived soon after. You were the only person missing. I think we all felt it but couldn't bring ourselves to mention you.

Val and her boyfriend came once we were back home. She walked into the bedroom, took one look at Daniel and me and broke out into the biggest smile. Then we both burst into tears. I don't know . . . all this crying over something that happens every second of every day.

After she'd gone, I fed Daniel and he dozed off in the crook of my arm. Lots of flowers have been delivered to our flat and it's very hot with the central heating. I drifted off to sleep taking in the heavy scent of lilies and roses. At some point James must have joined us too, and I woke to find him snuggled up next to me. I heard the sound of children playing outside, and I wondered what's in store for us as a family.

I don't know what I think about eternal life, or if I can even start to think about what that means. Oh, I know what I'm supposed to 'believe' now I'm a Christian; I'm supposed to be full of joy, and certain that I'm going to heaven. And according to many of my fellow believers I'm supposed to be full of joy that I'm going there, even if thousands or millions are going to hell.

But lying there in the dark listening to the steady breathing of my husband and my son I thought if there is just one moment we could pick, just one, to hold us safe in eternity, this would be it.

> *Your loving daughter,*
> *Ruth*

* * * *

January 29th

I'm walking down the high street proudly pushing little Daniel in his pram. It's 10 a.m. and this stroll has become part of my daily routine while James is at home looking for work.

As I walk past the supermarket, I glance at the bench under the tree. The elderly woman is there again. She's there at this time every day, as long as the weather's half decent.

The daytime world of my hometown is one that I never really thought about when I was getting on a train every morning to go to work. But as I take Daniel out and about, I'm starting to get to know people on the street and in the shops. I'm beginning to recognize the local 'characters' and the office workers as they go for their lunchtime sandwiches.

This lady on the bench has been catching my eye for a couple of weeks now. I keep getting the feeling that I should try to talk to her, but she looks so lost in her thoughts she might resent the intrusion.

Is this the Holy Spirit trying to tell me something, or just plain nosiness on my behalf? Whatever the reason, this morning I stop.

'I hope you don't mind us joining you here. It is a lovely spot,' I start cautiously as I arrange myself on the edge of the bench.

At first she looks up suspiciously. But soon her face breaks into a smile and she replies, 'Well, yes, it is.'

We start to talk. We talk about Daniel being my first baby, how I love being a mum, about lack of sleep and nappies, and how things were done in her day. About my husband being out of work at the moment, and how *I* haven't missed work at all.

Then suddenly she points down the road. 'My daughter used to work up there. Just part-time, mind you. She used to start at 10.30 a.m. and we used to meet on this bench right here most weekdays. We would just sit here and talk, really, before I went off for my morning shop and she went off to work.'

She stops for a moment and looks up at the sky.

'She died of breast cancer ten months ago now and I still come here, to our meeting place, nearly every day. I know it sounds odd, but I still talk to her in my head. I miss her so much.'

We sit in silence. Tears are rolling down my face, but the lady seems calm.

Sometimes I wonder why God doesn't just come back and wind it all up now. How could you ever get over something like that?

I think of the verse from Revelation: 'He will wipe every tear from their eyes . . .'[1]

But I want it for this woman sitting next to me *now*. I want it for everyone I've known or interviewed at work that has lost someone, be it a child to meningitis or a teenager to a car accident, or a brother or sister or mum or dad.

Will they see their loved-ones again, Lord? Even if they don't know you?

I look down at the tiny baby happily snoozing in his pram and think of his dad. I think I would just fall down and die if I ever lost either of them.

I've been given this child, this unbelievably precious gift – but with it comes the ever-present possibility of loss. I know that's what makes it so valuable, but I was never prepared for this pain I feel.

I look at the woman sitting next to me. Where is God in all this? Should I offer to pray for her? Talk about church and Jesus? There's absolutely nothing I can say that seems at all appropriate, so I pray in my head to the God who binds up the broken-hearted, and I pray that he will somehow comfort her.

For a while we just sit together, but soon the woman starts to get up. But she pauses, turns to me and simply says, 'Thank you for noticing me.'

And we go our separate ways.

* * * *

February 18th

'The redundancy money's going to run out soon, sweetheart.' James looks worried. I take his hand and squeeze it tightly.

It's early Monday evening and dusk is falling. We're walking on the local heath with our baby son in his pram.

This place is special to me. It's where I finally made a commitment to Jesus, and where I sometimes come to run and pray.

I've been trying to pray a bit more recently, with James being out of work for so long. I've actually been feeling more peaceful, especially after what happened at church yesterday, and I suddenly realize I haven't yet had the chance to tell James about the picture.

I start to talk but I'm making very little sense. I've got baby-brain, and the days and nights are starting to blur into one.

'Picture?' my husband says, slightly confused. 'As in "words" and "pictures"?'

'Well, yes. But a real picture as well. They gave me a real picture at the Alpha Mums' coffee morning this week.'

James nods. He's still with me, just about. I've been helping out with Alpha Mums, and I tell him that on Saturday the visiting speaker gave us all postcards with paintings on the front as part of his talk.

The picture on mine shows an older-looking man comforting a small child in his arms. The man looks kind and has massive hands.

I delve deep into my handbag, discarding various baby accessories, and fish out the postcard to show to James. He studies it and grins back at me. 'Very nice, sweetheart, but I've got a feeling there's more.'

I nod and carry on. 'Well, you know I went to the front at church yesterday for prayer while you looked after Daniel? A young woman came up to me and said she had a picture for me. And she described perfectly the scene on the postcard you're holding in your hands. I'm kind of getting the feeling God might be trying to tell me something. I'm hoping it means that we shouldn't have to worry about the future, about a job for you. After all, God knows how it's all going to turn out in the end.'

But even as the words leave my mouth a shudder of fear runs through me. What's going on here?

The image of God comforting a child in his arms should be reassuring but instead I'm suddenly wondering how it all works. How can God know our beginnings and our ends? How on earth did he 'arrange' the postcard/picture thing? And why is this all suddenly making me feel scared?

I feel the cold of the early evening and pull my coat tighter around me. I've been here before. I remember the Alpha course I went on and the endless debates and discussions about free will, predestination and time.

We're nearing the end of our walk now. I tell James what I'm thinking, and he smiles at me.

'Ruth, it really is pointless trying to understand how God works. Even the cleverest scholar will never be able to fathom eternity – our brains just aren't wired to take it in. We are created beings and we just can't imagine being outside time.'

I start to talk but James carries on, 'You make it so complicated and it's not. Jesus tells us to receive the kingdom like little children and then go and tell other people. Look again.' My husband brandishes the Alpha speaker's postcard. 'It's God the Father and he's cradling you in his arms. It's that simple.'

Is that really all I need to know? But I'm tired. I'm tired of stressing about jobs and money, and I don't want the worry to spoil the precious first months of our son's life. I'm tired of trying to stay positive to be a good 'witness' to our non-Christian friends.

When everything else is stripped away it just comes down to this: Does God, this being that we literally can't get our heads round, really care about the details of our little lives? When it all gets too much, can we crawl into his arms and be safe?

My husband's phone rings as we reach the car, and as he answers, Daniel starts to stir in his pram. I pick up my baby and hold him tight.

* * * *

April 9th

'So, Ruth, how's it going at that church of yours? Exorcised any demons recently?' My friend Val carefully places her coffee cup on the table and looks up at me, her face a picture of innocence.

Oh help.

She only said she was popping round for a cup of coffee and a catch-up. Discussions about spiritual warfare were certainly not on the agenda and I'm not sure I'm up for this today.

I reply weakly, 'Flip, Val, where did that come from?'

She smiles. 'Well, dear friend, I've finally realized this evangelical Christianity lark is not just a passing fad for you, so I decided to do a bit of research. It's amazing what you can find out in a couple of hours on the Web. Wikipedia was especially helpful and it told me that your church believes in – how did they put it? – casting out demons. Not the sort of thing I remember from my Sunday school days, but there you go.'

I open my mouth, ready to talk about people carrying around unhelpful burdens, but Val's enjoying herself and carries on.

'Well, it's all very interesting. Apparently quite a few evangelicals don't believe that Barack Obama is a real Christian because he's probably a universalist and thinks everyone ends up in heaven. We've been friends for a long time now, so I thought it would be interesting to see what you think about certain issues. Are you up for it?'

I'm not sure where Val's going here, and I'm pretty sure it could end in tears. Is this going to be a faith-sharing opportunity or a hostile grilling?

I gulp down some coffee, and groan. 'Yes, go ahead.'

Val looks pleased and produces a notebook from her handbag. 'OK, I'll start with a nice easy one. Do you believe that homosexuality is a sin?'

'Oh yes, a very simple question. And my answer is that I don't know.'

'Really? What about heaven and hell? Who goes where?'

'I don't know.'

'Are you a universalist like the president?'

'I'd like to be, but there's a very inconvenient quote in the Bible by Jesus who said, 'I am the way and the truth and the life. No-one comes to the Father except through me.'[2] Val sighs and continues, 'So you believe that Hindus and Muslims don't get to heaven?'

'I don't know.'

'What about people like me who don't go to church? Where do I end up?'

'Val, I don't *know*!'

'You're not a very good convert to evangelical Christianity, are you? Let's change tack slightly – what are your views on Harry Potter and Philip Pullman?'

'Val, you know I love the Harry Potter books, and we went together to see the play of Pullman's books and it was brilliant. What's going on here?'

She frowns. 'I'm just trying to check the extent of your brainwashing. But I have to say I'm slightly disappointed. You don't seem to believe what you're supposed to.'

Now my head's starting to hurt. All I want to do is to be a good witness. Val and I are glaring at each other across the table. It's not supposed to be like this – is it?

Why does it matter so much what I believe about heaven, hell and homosexuality? I still belong to Jesus – shouldn't I just be talking about him?

Val's still ranting. 'That's what really gets me about you lot – you think you've got the monopoly on God. Based on what you've just told me, a lot of your church friends would doubt that you are a true Christian. I know *I'm* not a Christian in your eyes. But I pray. Actually, I pray quite a lot. I pray for the people I interview at work. I pray for friends and family. I've even prayed for *you* before, if you must know. Who says I'm not praying to exactly the same God as you are?'

I start to laugh. Val prays. But of course she does. And now I'm completely stumped.

'Val, will you just let me tell you what I do believe – and why?'

She sighs again. 'Only if you try very hard not to patronize me.'

I've been waiting a long time for this moment. I send up a silent prayer for help – and begin.

'OK, do you remember when I took some time off work and went to India?'

Val nods. 'Yes. You were miserable, and you wanted to find yourself.'

'That's right. But I came back even more lost. I don't think I was depressed in the clinical sense, but I felt wretched. I was walking around with a sick feeling in my stomach and it wouldn't go away. Anyway, a few months later I was in Poland with work and something just snapped. I stumbled into the back of a church and cried. And then I called out to God, the Christian God, to help me, and said if he did I would try to find him.'

As I'm talking I remember it so clearly. The cold winter evening, the priest lighting the candles . . . and then falling to my knees.

I look up at Val. 'And God did help me. And that was the start of it. Something happened, and a few years later I found the church James and I go to now.'

Val sighs. 'Yes, great. So going to church helped you and gave you something to take your mind off things when you were feeling low. That's fine. If it had been me I'd have just painted the bathroom, but there you go.'

This is not the reaction I'd hoped for. 'Oh, please don't be flippant, Val.'

'I'm not. Not all of us are walking around with inner sickness or whatever you called it just now. Look, I believe in God and

I pray. But do you really want to know what stops me going to church? It's the people in it. I don't want to join the "gang", all love thy neighbour, then they're down the road sniping, bitching and thinking they're better than everyone else.'

I feel sick. 'Is that what you really think, Val? Is that what you think about James and me?'

'No, but let me tell you a story. When I was growing up, one of our neighbours went to a church like yours. Lovely man. One day he found out he had a brain tumour – suddenly people at his church were making out that it was some kind of judgement from God.'

'Well, I just don't believe that. He must have misunderstood.'

'Ruth, he didn't. And it's been my experience that Christians are self-absorbed people who are anti-gay, anti any other religions, and believe God damns people to hell.'

This kind of 'toxic Christian' rant is becoming all too familiar, and it's starting to depress me. I feel like banging my head on the table. This lovely woman has been such a good friend to me. I just want her to understand my faith.

'OK, I get the idea. But that hasn't been my experience. Let me tell you about Rosie at my church. Every Friday night she organizes a team of people who search out the homeless and – '

Val interrupts. 'Yes, Ruth. Lots of people do amazingly good things and they are not Christians. Some belong to different religions, and some don't believe in God at all.'

She's running rings round me. How am I going to get through? Suddenly I'm talking again. It's almost a surprise to hear my voice.

'Val, what keeps me at church is that I'm thankful. I believe that Jesus Christ turned my life around, and there's nothing I can ever do to repay him. And when I pray and when I worship something bypasses my brain and goes straight to my heart. I don't understand what happened on the cross – I don't think I'm meant to – but I believe I was rescued, and when I called on his name in that church in Poland something slowly started to happen. It was years later that I started to go to church, and some time after that when I finally made a commitment. But I've learnt that not only do I need Jesus in my life, I absolutely believe he holds everything – including me – together.'

I look at my friend. For once she is speechless. And I wonder what on earth is going on inside her head.

* * * *

June 19th

The cheer is almost deafening. James has just announced to our cell group that he's finally found a job.

'Well, thank goodness for that! We can all stop fasting now,' the leader laughs.

Is he joking? I peer nervously at the waistlines of the people around me. My husband was out of work for a long time . . .

'So how do you feel now? Anything you'd like to share about your experiences?' I realize the group leader is talking to us.

James and I look at each other and my husband starts, 'I'm not sure we've got any particular spiritual insight. In a way, we just had to get on with things. We really didn't have a choice. I applied for jobs and didn't get them, and we kept trying to believe that God was with us and kept praying, really.'

Hmmm. It would be great to look back and be proud of the way we dealt with it all, but I'm not sure I passed with flying colours. I've been so churned up, so up and down.

I begin to talk, but only manage 'We're just so relieved . . .' before bursting into tears.

Oh, how embarrassing. I really hate losing it like this, but it's happened quite a lot since I started going to church.

During the Alpha course we attended, I'm sure I listened to most of the talks with a strange grimace on my face as I desperately tried to stop the tears from falling.

When I asked the Alpha teacher why I was reacting like this, she said gently, 'I think it might be that you're feeling the presence of God.'

Well, I don't think I'm feeling God's presence now. I'm just extremely embarrassed.

'What's the matter with me? Why can't I get a grip? People have been through much worse stuff than this,' I mumble, as Jenny, one of the leaders, quickly steers me into the room next door where our baby is sleeping in his pushchair.

I should be happy tonight. But I can't shake the helplessness I felt each time another job opportunity came to nothing. Watching my normally optimistic husband struggle with hurt and disappointment made me realize what's in store for me as a mother. I can't protect my husband or my son from the bad stuff in life.

I look up at Jenny and start to explain, 'There was nothing I could do apart from pray, and most of the time God was the last thing on my mind. And just recently my worries have been spiralling out of control.'

'Let it all out Ruth, just talk to me,' she says.

So I do. I tell her that I'm so tired, that I'm worrying about everything and I'm terrified that something really bad is going to happen to my husband or our baby.

'I've been reading Psalm 91 for comfort, but I know that terrible things happen to Christians and non-Christians alike. I can hardly watch the news at the moment without getting into a state. I used to be tougher than this; I used to *write* the news, for crying out loud!'

Jenny interrupts. 'OK, stop right there, Ruth. We're going to pray. God has given you this baby and your husband – for however long *he* decides. You can't control this; you've got to give it up to him.'

We start to pray, and in my mind I hand back my husband and my baby – the most precious things in my life that are not mine to own or keep, and never were.

After a while, Jenny takes out her notebook. 'Ben and I were at a conference last week and we heard this. I think it's a bit special, and we were going to share it tonight.'

The room seems very still as she starts to read: 'God is ultimately in control. God is there, whether I feel him or not. God has a plan for my life, whether I understand it or not. God works in the way he chooses (the best way), whether I like it or not.'

This is so helpful I want to hug her. It's somehow so comforting, and immediately I know I'm going to sleep well tonight. And I suddenly wonder if in a few years' time we'll look back on all this and thank God for his perfect timing.

* * * *

Sunday, 8 p.m.

Dear Dad,
Well, a big relief. And that's the thing about God (if you believe in him, of course) – you never really know what he's up to.

I've been trying to get more to grips with my faith recently, and do some reading and studying. So far I've learnt that Jesus is quite keen on breaking rules and getting people to work things out for themselves.

So I'm trying to learn more about how God works. I'm praying more too, and have joined a group of mums who study the Bible together.

I'm watching, listening and trying to 'increase' my faith, but the more I think about it, the more bemused I get.

If I'm being very honest, the resurrection confuses me and the Trinity baffles me. I also worry about heaven, hell, and what God does all day if he's outside time.

And don't get me started on the Old Testament.

71

I'm actually starting to think there's something wrong with me. I was in crèche this morning and the Bible story was Noah and the ark.

All the mums were sitting sweetly with their little ones and singing songs about the animals going into the ark, but all I could think about was the people and animals that didn't make it. Were all the people who drowned wicked? All of them – even the babies and children who died? Thousands of entire families just wiped out. Did they deserve that? And yes, I've heard the argument that humankind had – and has – been tainted or contaminated by sin and that God is holy and just, but I'm not convinced that God 'has' to act in a certain way. After all, he's God, isn't he? I'm not sure I want the God who acts on an angry, vengeful whim.

Up until now I've just brushed aside these kinds of questions and kept going. I think our church's definition of this is holding things 'in tension'. But this morning I was looking at Daniel and wondered, what am I going to tell him when he's older? Do I tell him I believe in a genocidal God, or a God who'll find you a parking space if you pray, but who allows unbearable suffering to happen daily? That not everyone goes to heaven?

I need to get this sorted – because one day that baby with the big blue eyes is going to ask me what I believe.

Yet again my faith is being put sharply into focus. How can I get beyond this?

Tuesday, 2 p.m.

I'm not really certain about anything at the moment. A lot of Christians I've come across are very sure about what they believe and are very sure that they are right.

And some of them are not just sure they're right – they want you to agree with them. Gideon from cell group, for example. He was insisting last week that there is only one interpretation of the Bible, that it's very clear and consistent. When I said a lot of the Bible confused me, he said I was looking for difficulties that didn't exist . . . that I just had to look at it his way. But of course.

Val's been very quiet since our discussion about God and the church, but last night she rang in a bit of a state.

'Have you got the radio on?' she barked.

'Yes, I have, actually. I'm listening to a Christian station and they're debating why 20- and 30-somethings don't go to church anymore. Apparently they're called the missing generation.'

'Well, switch over to Five Live and you'll find your answer. There's a man who claims to be a Christian saying God's bringing judgement on this country because we're so accepting of gay people. And that's my description; his way of putting it wasn't very nice. What kind of God would do that?' she said. 'I certainly wouldn't want to meet him, that's for sure.'

So, Dad, it seems some people actually prefer the Old Testament God. I hope Neil wasn't listening too.

It's not rocket science, is it? If church is seen as a place of judgement and rules rather than a place of compassion and safety, people are not going to come through our doors.

Thursday, 7 p.m.

I'm sorry if I've been ranting over the last few days. One of the mums at Bible study reckons I'm wrestling with God. Perhaps I'm feeling unsettled because James is now back at work and I'm on my own during the day. But I'm still plugged into church life, and I'm trying to immerse myself in spiritual things. I'm searching for answers. And I've been praying I'll finally get some closure on my issues with the Old Testament God.

This morning's reading in my Bible notes was Jesus talking about how he is the Good Shepherd, and this was a big relief to me. No trace of a remote, harsh God here. Jesus cares for every one of his sheep and knows them by name. He knows them and he loves them, and they know him.

And while I'm thinking about love, I've got to tell you this – baby Daniel sat up on his own for the first time today. He looked at me with such pride on his face, and I thought my heart would burst.

Dad, I never expected all this to happen to me. I never thought I'd be a wife to someone I love so much, and a mum. I never knew I would love my baby like this, and that sometimes that love would feel almost unbearable.

Is this how God feels about us? How you and Mum felt when you had me and Neil?

When I go to Daniel in the middle of the night when he cries, I want to make him feel safe. I sometimes say, 'Mummy's here.' I hold him and tell him I'll always be here.

But I know I won't always be there for him, and more than ever now I want all the God stuff to be true. I want it to be true that he sent Jesus to die for us, whatever that means. I want Jesus to be the Good Shepherd.

I cannot believe that all this wonder and joy mixed with pain and dread at the thought of losing all that I hold precious, is somehow meaningless.

I need to know there is hope and this isn't all a horrible accident.

Friday, midday

OK, so what do you make of this? This morning I was listening to Christian radio and the reading was . . . The Good Shepherd. And then I went to my friend's house for coffee and the exact verse was on her fridge. 'I am the Good Shepherd.'

I love it when this happens. It's nothing earth-shattering, neither is it a deeply profound revelation, and yes, it could be complete coincidence. But I'm going to take it as a simple answer to prayer. Perhaps this is what people mean when they say 'God told me this.' And I'm not entirely sure what it is that God's telling me, but when I got home I turned up the radio in the kitchen, picked up my baby and danced for joy.

I'm still not sure exactly what I believe, but I'm going to say it anyway. God is on my side and he is good.

Your loving daughter,

Ruth

PART FOUR:

MAKING MUSIC

September 9th

'Chocolate?' My friend Jo frowns. 'You gave up chocolate? How did *that* help anyone?'

I'm at a coffee shop with two mums I know from antenatal classes, and I'm wondering why on earth I opened my mouth. But I've started the story now, so I guess I'd better get on with it.

'Look, I know you're going to find this hard to believe. I can understand that.'

As I sip my coffee, the women exchange glances. I suppose I should be used to odd looks by now. I often get this reaction when I talk about my faith. Perhaps I should avoid the subject altogether – my recent attempts at evangelism have hardly been successful.

It would be fair to say that my attempt a while back at 'sharing' my faith with Val definitely fell on rocky ground. And last week my offer to pray for my brother's sore neck was firmly rejected when he jumped halfway across the room, shouting, 'Go away, you weirdo.'

Now Jo and Delphine are shifting uncomfortably in their seats. I start again.

'I'm not explaining this very well, am I? Just let me go back to the beginning. We knew this couple from church; in fact we were in the same cell group.'

'Cell group?' Delphine looks worried. Great, now I've actually started speaking like a Christian. I remember when 'church talk' was a foreign language to me.

'Sorry. Nothing to do with prisons. It's a bit like a prayer meeting and a Bible study combined so you get to know the people pretty well. Anyway, this couple had been trying for a baby for quite a while and had recently had a miscarriage. They'd been so excited and it was just awful. I really wanted to do something, so I decided to give up chocolate for Lent. I know that sounds so trivial compared to what they were going through, and of course I didn't tell them what I was doing. But the idea was that every time I thought of chocolate, I'd pray for a baby for them. I would have done more but I was still breastfeeding so it seemed the best I could do. I'm kind of addicted to Dairy Milk, so there were lots of prayers going up, especially just before Easter. In fact I prayed and prayed, and lit candles in the Roman Catholic Church near the park once a week.'

I stop and look at my friends. Jo still looks doubtful but Delphine seems intrigued.

'So what happened, Ruth?' Delphine's voice is soft. 'Were your prayers answered?'

'Well, this is the bit you may find hard to believe. I'd given up chocolate all Lent and then on Easter Sunday, the woman I'd been praying for called me to ask if I'd swap duties in the crèche.

And she told me that she was pregnant, that she'd had an early scan and that everything looked fine.'

Jo interrupts, 'I'm sorry, did you say Easter Sunday?'

'Yes. Everything's going well for them, and the baby's due in December.'

I glance at my friends. They don't know where to look and I feel my cheeks redden.

Have I really just said that because I gave up chocolate for Lent, God gave this couple a much longed-for baby? And arranged for me to be told the news on Easter Sunday?

If someone had just told me that story, I'd be sceptical too.

I suddenly feel the need to explain. 'The chocolate's a red herring. I just prayed a lot, and I'm guessing that lots of other people were praying too. And on this occasion I believe our prayers were answered.'

I'm suddenly almost indignant. I really do believe God answered our prayers and I think it's pretty amazing.

As we prepare to leave, Delphine looks over at me and something about her expression seems familiar. It's as if she doesn't quite know what to make of what I've just said, that it seems potty, but that she knows me well enough to know I'm actually vaguely sane.

I smile as I realize that this used to be my reaction when church-going friends told me 'unbelievable' stories of healing and miracles.

I'm glad I opened my mouth a few minutes ago. I am a Christian now, and I don't want to be embarrassed about it.

I don't make friends that easily, though, and I love spending time with Jo and Delphine. I don't particularly want to be dropped because they think I'm odd.

Lord, I want to tell of all your deeds, but why does it have to be so hard?

* * * *

October 5th

'Yes, you! The lady with the buggy.' I'm at a Women's Day with my friend Olivia and I realize the lady at the front is talking to me.

We've just had some interesting teaching about hearing from God, and now it's time for a practical 'prophecy' demonstration.

I'm very excited to be picked on, and lean forward so I can hear every word.

'I got a very strong feeling when you walked in,' the woman smiles. 'Something connected to making music. And I've just had an image of an instrument in my mind. An oboe. Does that mean anything to you?'

Crikey. 'Well, yes. I did play the oboe as a child.' Several people start to clap but I interrupt. 'I wasn't very good at it, though. In fact, I think my music teacher used to despair of me.'

The room erupts in laughter. I'm slightly bewildered and start to protest, but Olivia gives me a sharp nudge in the ribs and the woman at the front carries on: 'I think the Lord is saying that it's time for you to make music again.'

Again? It's highly debatable whether I ever made music in the first place. But I guess that's not the point. I sit back and try to digest what's just happened.

There are more 'words' and 'pictures' being directed at other people now, but no one looks particularly fazed. In fact, they almost seem to expect it. I wonder whether this will ever all be 'normal' to me. And for the first time since I became a Christian I wonder if I'd be better off at a church where this kind of stuff just doesn't happen.

At least then my head would hurt less.

As we walk to the main hall for a worship session, Olivia asks how I felt about the musical 'word'.

'It's odd, but half of me is completely bowled over and the other half is wondering why all this stuff has to be so *weird*. It's almost like the mind-readers I used to write about for the newspaper.'

I love talking to my friend Olivia – I can always be completely honest with her. She's been a Christian for a long time and always seems to find the right words to reassure me.

As we take our seats she says, 'Well, yes, it is weird to you as a citizen of this country at this particular time in history. But a lot of cultures around the world haven't yet dumped their spiritual sides and would just accept it. I imagine all that psychic stuff you used to cover was a lot stranger than what happened just now, and I'm willing to bet they charged good money for their consultations.'

Of course they did. There's really no comparison. And it strikes me that perhaps part of me doesn't want this to become normal, because that's when I cross a line and really leave my old self behind. Maybe I'm still trying to keep a foot in both camps.

The band starts up and I close my eyes and just listen for a while. The singer is amazing. She's not grabbing attention, but her voice is beautiful and it makes me want to sing my heart out. And suddenly the air seems thick with the presence of God.

Lord, thank you. Thank you for blessing me with a word, thank you for this day, for my friend Olivia, thank you for this wonderful music.

Lord, I want to make music for you in my life, I really do. I want to be open to you and the way you work. I want to switch my spiritual side back on.

And I lift my voice . . .

I've got to remember this; I want to treasure this moment, this lovely day. Because, for me at least, being a Christian is not always straightforward. It's like I'm trying to grasp something that I can never quite catch. Sometimes it just seems that if I blink I'll miss it, and I wonder if I've imagined those special times when God seems close and everything seems to make sense.

Sometimes. But not today.

* * * *

December 11th

'But should churches ever close their doors?' We're sitting round the table at cell group debating whether a deadly strain of flu will sweep the world this winter.

Our leader, Ben, pauses and consults his laptop. 'Well, a flu expert says here that in the next few years we can expect a "really major epidemic" in the northern hemisphere. Churches may well be asked to shut down to stop the virus spreading, but in my view they shouldn't. We may get a lot of frightened people at our door needing comfort. And what a great opportunity to really get out there and minister to the sick.'

He seems to be relishing the prospect of a disaster, maybe a little too much for my liking. Perhaps he doesn't realize what the consequences could be.

'Well, I'd be more than a bit worried about what could happen in the crèche if we did stay open,' I say, and the image of my own little boy pops into my head. 'I mean, what would happen if someone ignored symptoms and came in anyway? This is serious stuff; one of the children could die.'

'Absolutely yes, it is serious,' Ben says. 'And it would be a fantastic way for us to really be Christ to people who have lost loved ones, as Ruth was just saying.'

Hang on a second! I didn't say that at all. Perhaps I haven't made myself clear and he's just giving me the benefit of the doubt. Or does he just see the best in people so much that he's actually completely misheard?

I often wonder about the niceness of Christians, of people at our church who really don't have a critical word to say.

Surely even godly people need to let off steam. Do they ever go home and explode to their spouse, flatmates or pets? I imagine Ben raging around the kitchen, 'That Ruth Roberts, I am getting so fed *up* with her! Is she ever going to *learn*?'

I shift uncomfortably in my seat. 'Actually Ben, that's not what I meant at all. My first thought was not about helping people, it was about my baby catching the bug.'

Ben's wife, Jenny, smiles at me. 'That's because you're a mother, Ruth.'

What a lovely thing to say. I realize I really do want to be more like these people who can always find a gentle and comforting, helpful word. I can be open and honest with them and feel brave to say what's really on my mind.

'OK, but I am serious about the crèche. How far do we put ourselves and our families at risk? Would it be God's will for me to knowingly take my child to an infectious area? When we deliberately ignore medical advice on not going to church, aren't we doing the same as people who stop taking vital medicines and pray for healing instead? It would be like deliberately putting my hand in a tub of boiling water. Would God ask me to do that? And I'd be stupid to put my hand in while praying for protection, wouldn't I? Or, perhaps I'll just *trust* that when I turn out of this road there won't be a car coming the other way. I mean, come on, God has given me a brain as well.'

Ben looks sad. 'I'm sorry, Ruth, but this is something you'd have to work out between you and God. It's something that maybe we're all going to have to think about in the coming months.'

The room falls silent, and I think about the ten or so mums in the church crèche, and the horrific prospect that one of their children wouldn't make it through the winter.

One in ten . . . the words swim round my head and suddenly my memory transports me to an ill-equipped medical centre in a different part of the world. I picture myself furiously tapping away at a television script: 'In the poorest areas of the poorest countries, one in ten children will die before reaching their fifth birthday.' And it dawns on me that this 'disaster' scenario is already being played out daily in parts of Africa I've visited with work.

I think of the mothers I met who had lost their children to AIDS, malaria, or even dehydration. They were full of grief and sorrow. But not fear.

And I pray for even a fraction of their courage.

* * * *

March 3rd

'So Ruth, do you think the Lord is with us absolutely everywhere, or are there some places he wouldn't be able to follow?'

I'm walking in the park with Charlotte, my husband's teenage cousin. It's a beautiful, sunny afternoon and I'm pushing Daniel in his buggy. Today it's easy to believe that Jesus is right beside us.

'I'm not sure, Charlotte. Why do you ask?'

'Well, I was at youth group last week and we were talking about the presence of God, and if Jesus were physically alive today whether he'd be able to enter somewhere like an abortion clinic. You know, when they actually go down and have their operations. Or is abortion such a terrible sin that a holy God would have to withdraw?'

My legs almost give way. I regain my balance and tightly grip the pushchair handle. Charlotte looks at me. 'Are you OK, Ruth?'

'I think so . . .' It's the most honest answer I can give at the moment, and I think about what she's just said.

It's a good question, an interesting theological debating point, I'm sure. But it's thrown me back to a dark time in my past, and I wonder – was Jesus with me when I went down for my 'operation' all those years ago?

I look at Charlotte. She's so young and fervent in her faith. She's probably trying to work out why I've gone quiet – but I don't know what to say.

What can I tell her? Where would I start? As I think back to the morning of that dreadful day, I picture the faces of the women I encountered at the clinic. I see the doctor who tried to persuade me to change my mind, her features hardening to resignation as I shook my head. The women in the packed waiting room, heads bent, their eyes dull and lifeless. The girl opposite me, who couldn't have been more than 14, with her mum and dad sitting on either side. All three were crying.

I remember feeling so sorry for them, but knew that what I was about to do wouldn't affect me, that I was tougher than that. Just a minor blip, and then I'd be able to get back to normal, back on track. But I cried when I woke up from my operation, and when Val came to pick me up I could hardly talk. Later, when I closed my eyes and tried to sleep, it felt like falling into nothingness.

The tears still come easily and I stare up at the sky, trying to blink them away. I'm suddenly longing to see the pastors at our church. I'm longing for their reassurance, and accept-ance.

So, could a holy God be present in the abortion clinic? I look again at the young girl walking quietly beside me.

There's so much I want to say to her. That I just don't know whether he was there or not, and I'm not sure that's the point. That I think it's more about mercy, compassion and the tender way God deals with us. That to me it's about how his people treated a woman who was broken inside, and gently steered her towards the cross.

I want to tell her how, when I eventually started to go to church, I felt like a condemned woman as I waited for the subject of abortion to come up.

Then one day it did. And I was bracing myself for some kind of onslaught when a young man took the microphone and said there was someone here who'd had an abortion and that God wanted to forgive them. That God loved them. And it was all said in such a gentle way.

Charlotte, please stay close to God. He is the God of second chances and when the time came it was easy for me to fall to my knees. But please don't go there. Because even though I am start-ing to get my head round the fact that my debt has been paid by Jesus, I still have to live with who I've been and what I've done.

But I say nothing. Instead I bend down to stroke my son's velvety smooth head, and wonder what became of all those women in the waiting room.

* * * *

May 4th

I'm jogging along the riverbank near my home, and as I round a corner I almost run straight into a teenage boy skimming stones into the water. He mutters an apology, while the older woman he's with glares at him as if it's entirely his fault.

They look so similar she has to be his mum, and as I set off on my run again I glance back. They're both staring into space looking thoroughly awkward, and I suddenly feel the urge to pray for them.

I used to do this sort of thing all the time when I was a very new Christian. I'd pray for people in my head as I walked down the street – 'Lord, please help that couple have a great evening, give that man something to smile about, send that lonely-looking girl a friend.'

So now I ask God to bring the mother and son closer together, and to bless their relationship so they'll have some fun this morning. And as I pray I feel the warmth of the sun on my skin. I suddenly notice the sparkle of the spring sunshine on the water, and I smile with delight.

Why don't I do this more? I used to pray a lot. On my train journey to work I'd write down all my requests and a long list of people to pray for. Then I'd pray for all my fellow passengers in the carriage; that they'd have a good day and that God would draw them closer to him. Quietly, in my head of course; I didn't want to get arrested.

Perhaps I was a little bit naïve, but I really did expect God to hear me – and answer. Doesn't Jesus say that if you believe, you will receive whatever you ask for in prayer?

I smile as I remember that I'd sometimes even pray for the Holy Spirit to come now and fill the train carriage – and then scan the passengers for evidence of his appearance.

Was it just my overactive imagination, or was the woman who'd been so engrossed in her newspaper now gazing out of the window with a peaceful look on her face?

Or did the red-faced man in a suit *really* look startled, and spin round as if someone had just tapped him on the shoulder?

I fix my eyes on the path ahead and wonder what happened to all that passion and enthusiasm. Well, I'm still a new mum, I guess, and I've been busy – busy with our little boy, tired, and maybe a bit too absorbed in our family unit.

I've got a funny feeling I've left something vital behind. I know I've got less time now, but there must be more I could do.

Suddenly I remember our pastor's 'take' on serving – that we should just do what we can. Well, I've just reminded myself of what I can easily do.

I've reached the spot in my run where the river intersects with the main road into town, and I stop and watch as car after car whizzes by. I start to pray. I pray for all those people in the cars; I pray that God will somehow touch their lives today. And I pray that if they don't know him, then they'll start to seek his presence.

I'm in full flow when I'm startled by the sound of laughter. It could be my imagination again, but it sounded a lot like the low-pitched chuckle of a teenage boy.

So I turn round and there's the mother and son, except now there's smiles and chatter, and as they walk past they seem happy in each other's company.

Was that an answer to prayer? How will I ever know? I never even knew the beginning of the story, let alone the end.

But I'm not supposed to be privy to the mind of God, am I? It's not for me to know his purposes and his plans. I'm just supposed to pray – and what's the point in praying if you don't believe your prayers are going to be answered?

Could it really be as simple as that? I take one last look at the cars speeding past me, and start a slow jog home.

* * * *

May 15th

I'm standing next to James in church and I'm starting to break out in a cold sweat. A very large and slightly scary image of our son is looming above us on the overhead screen, but that's the least of our worries.

Sitting directly behind us is Val and her boyfriend, and next to them is Neil, who only managed two songs the last time before running out in terror.

I remind myself that, no, it's not a bad dream; our little boy is just about to be dedicated as part of the Sunday morning service – hence the family, friends and giant picture of Daniel.

The real thing is in my arms, squirming, while James and I desperately try to clean up his cute but crusty nose.

We're in the middle of a worship song and I nervously scan the room. I know I shouldn't be worrying about how my non-believing friends and family are reacting to being here, but I can't help it. I'm strangely torn between feeling overprotective of our church, and at the same time mildly embarrassed because I know how weird all this can look to outsiders. And sure enough, just across the aisle from Val a man is worshipping his heart out. He's really going for it with his eyes closed and arms punching the air.

Val catches my eye and gives me a strange 'Ooh, would you look at him' kind of look. In the past we might have giggled together, but now I just want to tell her to behave.

I know she misses the 'old Ruth' and has really given me a hard time since I became a Christian. She's quizzed me mercilessly about my beliefs, and I remember how she shouted 'hypocrite' at me in the crowded restaurant. Well, now she can finally see what all the fuss is about.

The song ends and it's time for a break before the dedication starts. Val taps me on the shoulder and smiles. 'Well, that was interesting. But don't fret, I've seen it all before.'

I raise my eyebrows and she carries on, 'I went to the local Baptist church a few times and it was similar. People I thought were sensible were prancing around in some kind of rapture. It was really rather odd.'

Well, that's typical Val. Hang on a minute. Val's been to church? An *evangelical* church? When? But I don't have time for this now. The dedication starts soon, and my main concern should be trying to control our wriggly son as our pastor tries to bless him.

I look at Val and my brother sitting quietly next to her, and my heart sinks. Surely they're meant to come to church and at least experience the presence of God in some shape or form?

Neil does look a bit glassy-eyed but that's more likely a Sunday morning hangover than a reaction to the Holy Spirit.

What's going on, Lord? Why is being here so difficult for them? And am I really supposed to be trying to win them for you? Because I wouldn't know where to start.

We're preparing to go up to the front when I hear Neil say to Val, 'Well, at least we'll never have to come back here again'.

But instead of feeling hurt I start to smile. My husband and I have a little secret that we haven't told anyone yet, and sooner than they think we may very well be back here – with a new face on the overhead screen.

I need to leave Val and Neil to God's perfect timing, and concentrate on what we're about to do.

So we walk up to publicly say 'Thank you' for our precious son, and promise to help him know Jesus.

It's the best we can do.

* * * *

Monday, 8 p.m.

Dear Dad,
I'm sorry you weren't at the dedication. You would have enjoyed it. But I don't know how you would have reacted to what happened after the sermon. One of the leaders took

the microphone and said she wanted to pray for physical healing. She took time to explain to people that as Christians, we believe it's our job to heal the sick in the power of the Holy Spirit. And soon other church members walked up and started naming ailments they thought people needed to be healed from.

As conditions were called out, people in the congregation got up and picked their way to the front to be prayed for.

I looked at my friends and family members who don't go to church, and I didn't know whether to laugh or cry.

To someone who'd not seen this before it could have looked like a new type of godly game show: 'Painful hips and leg joints? Asthma? Come on down!'

At least Neil and Val knew what to expect. Janet's husband had never been to what I call a 'lively' church before. When our cell group leader took the microphone and said 'women's problems', he went bright red and looked a bit faint.

Later, at our dedication party, Val and Neil went outside to have a cigarette and I watched them through the window. They were clutching glasses of wine and shouting 'Cataracts!' and 'Gout!' to the bemusement of passers-by.

I'm not embarrassed about what happened. I'm still not entirely convinced about healings and miracles, even though I think I've seen a few myself. I do still sometimes feel like the man who shouted, 'Lord, help my unbelief!'[1]

But I am frustrated – yet again – by the seemingly insurmountable differences between the world inside and the world outside the church.

Jesus said he came for the sick and not the healthy, so good for Val and Neil if they don't need a doctor.[2]

Perhaps they would have thought twice though if a specific condition had been named and they'd been really suffering with it.

Wednesday, 8 p.m.

I keep thinking about Sunday, and healing.

And I'm remembering when the newspaper I worked for went through a phase of sending reporters to psychics and faith healers.

I was sent to a 'spiritual doctor' to see if he could help my painful shoulder. I wrote my piece and didn't think any more about it. That is, until the postbags started to arrive at my desk (it was a long time ago now and before emails). It was the biggest ever response to a news story I'd written. Each bag contained hundreds of letters from people all over the country. I remember reading them, and as I did my hands began to shake.

A little boy was dying of cancer, would the spiritual healer see him? Please could I help, they were going to lose him, they'd tried everything . . . A 10-year-old girl was in a coma, could the healer visit her in hospital? Could he help an 80-year-old lady's hip – she was in agony, the doctors had been trying their best, but . . .

They were mostly letters from readers who had been suffering with illnesses to varying degrees, or concerned and sometimes desperate relatives.

93

I had no faith in the healer, but I phoned him anyway. He complained that since the article had appeared he'd been inundated and would I tell all of these people he was too busy. I wanted to rip his head off.

Jesus would have seen the little boy with the leukemia, the girl, the grandma. Jesus would have healed them. In the Gospels he always did. But sometimes today he doesn't always seem to show up. I want to believe, Dad. I don't want to be negative about this stuff.

Lord, please help my unbelief!

Monday, 2 p.m.

Life has changed so much for me since I started to come to church, and now it's going to change again.

My identity has always been so tied up with work; journalist, and then a journalist on a mass-circulation tabloid, and now a journalist on one of the most popular TV shows in the country. Sounds good? Well, if I'm being honest, I like to think so.

I've already gone back part-time; we've just moved out of our flat into a house, and now there's another baby on the way I should probably stay at work until I go on maternity leave again.

But today I quit. Not because I have strong views on working mothers but because I miss my little boy more than I'm enjoying my job, and I guess I'm lucky enough to have this option.

James and I have been talking about it for a while, but I finally decided yesterday at church.

I was sitting quietly during the worship, thinking about how I would feel if my 'identity' changed to 'Mum at Home', and about the labels we give people generally.

Looking around the room I saw the lady who has Down's syndrome as she raised her arms in worship; the woman with an alcohol addiction, eyes tight shut and tears streaming down her face; and the solicitor, sitting (praying?) with his head in his hands.

Later, after Holy Communion I leafed through my Bible in search of inspiration, and found the postcard I'd been given at Alpha, of the man cradling the child in his arms.

On the back I'd written a Bible verse from Isaiah: 'Fear not, for I have redeemed you; I have summoned you by name; you are mine.'[3]

I'm not usually one to let myself go during worship, and you know I'm still cautious about my faith. But after taking the bread and wine you will always find me sitting quietly with tears dropping into my lap, and yesterday was no different. Not because I'm distressed or guilt-ridden or anything like that. I'm just remembering, saying thank you, and discovering who I am.

Friday, 9 p.m.

I've just got back from a late night dash to the supermarket to buy some crèche supplies for Sunday.

For some reason I've agreed to take on organizing 'craft' for the older children. What was I thinking? You would have thought that making a donkey 'template' for the Good Samaritan story would be a simple enough task, but apparently not. Donkeys are more difficult to draw than you might think. According to my usually kind husband, my donkey looked more like a horse. Then he tried, and if my donkey looked like a horse, his looked like a cow. Then we narrowly avoided arguing about why the Good Samaritan couldn't get carried away on a horse instead of a donkey. It's just not biblical, and I don't want to go there.

In the end, I resorted to printing a ready-made donkey from the Internet, but then realized I didn't have any glue. Or card.

I was minding my own business at the till, lost in my thoughts and wondering if perhaps people just don't need God in their lives any more, in this part of the world anyway.

Haven't most folk got everything more or less sorted? They love their families; yes they struggle sometimes, but they get by, make the best of it. Why would they need anything else?

Perhaps Jesus did just come for those who need him, not for those who think they don't.

But then a noise distracted me. The boy in the pushchair in front had dropped his toy and I bent down to pick it up. His mother was chatting to the pale supermarket worker checking items through the till.

I started to listen. Yes, he was tired, the man was saying. He worked all day in an office and then came here to do the

*late shift because it was the only way he could afford to pay
his mortgage after losing his well-paid job three years ago.
He shrugged his shoulders, then smiled and told the woman
he was looking forward to seeing* Singin' in the Rain *at the
weekend with his wife. Mustn't grumble and all that . . .*

*I glanced down at the magazines and newspapers at
the side of the till. 'Baby heartache for Hollywood star' one
headline screamed. Another story told how a footballer who
seemed to have everything had tried to take his own life.*

*Suddenly it felt like the room was spinning. I gazed round
the supermarket, taking in all the tired, stressed people, and
turned back just as a weary-looking woman at the next till
smacked her crying toddler.*

*It certainly wasn't how it's all presented in the adverts –
happy shoppers selecting products that would improve their
lives.*

*I did it again, Dad. I started to pray in my head for every-
one around me; the tired parents, the struggling till worker;
yes, even the celebrities on the front pages. Crazy?*

*Perhaps, but if there is a God and we are his children this
may be the only thing I can do.*

> *Your loving daughter,*
> *Ruth*

PART FIVE:

LITTLE CHILDREN

June 11th

I'm in the newsroom in my last few weeks at work, and my colleague Stephanie is bending my ear about a religious broadcast she's heard.

'So these vicars were having a right blast at the national newspapers for not reporting the imminent visit of a major religious leader. They were saying it was disgusting that the newspapers had ignored the story and that the television news programmes *had* covered it – as if there was some kind of hidden agenda. It made me so cross I started shouting at the radio.'

I open my mouth to protest, but my friend Patricia steps in. 'I suppose a lot of people don't have any idea how these things work, that it's easy for TV producers to preview stuff because they have the pictures on file, and that newspapers hardly ever report the news until it actually happens.'

'Unless it's a quiet news day, of course,' I say, and Stephanie manages a wry smile.

'Yes, but why do they have to be so defensive? I'm fed up of taking calls from religious people moaning that we don't represent their agendas. It obviously doesn't occur to them that the mainstream media doesn't exist to cater for a minority.'

There's not a lot I can say to that – Stephanie's right. The vast majority of people in the UK are not Christians and do not go to church on a Sunday morning, or at any time.

'Well, Ruth, this will all be a distant memory soon, eh?' My boss, Mike, has stopped at my desk. I think he's still surprised I've resigned. 'Looking forward to a being a lady of leisure? I know what you mums do all day, sitting around drinking coffee and gossiping.'

I smile. It's definitely time to go.

'We were just haranguing Ruth about religion and the media,' Patricia tells Mike.

'Do you think we're anti-Christian in our coverage?'

He pulls up a chair. 'Well, we can't really afford to be. Do you know how many God-botherers work around here? There's Angie in IT, John the director – both born-agains. Ruth here, of course. And a fair few more.'

Really? I didn't know that. And now I come to think about it, Mike seems to know an awful lot about evangelical Christians. I wonder what his background is?

I look around at my colleagues. I know I'm probably being oversensitive, but I do get a bit miffed when Christians have a go at the press. To listen to some people, you'd think the media is some kind of evil empire – its mission to thwart the will of God and water down good Christian values.

I know very well that news judgements and values are complicated things; they change, and are difficult to pin down. And the media is far from perfect. But as far as I can see, it's made up of individuals trying to serve their clients – their viewers, listeners and readers – just as any other business would. And these days most of those 'clients' don't go to church and have little interest in church things.

'Hey, Ruth, what do you think of this?' Patricia's giggling. 'Mike reckons most of Jesus' disciples would actually have been *Sun* readers, if they'd been around today.'

Mike grins. 'Of course. Working men, no-nonsense fishermen. What else would they have read? Anyway, I'm not paying you to discuss the meaning of life – haven't you all got links to write?'

As my workmates return to their desks, I sit back and watch the bustle of the busy newsroom. These are all funny, clever, *kind* people. Do they need Jesus in their lives?

I look at John, whose father has just died; Nasim, who has a son with cerebral palsy; Marcella, whose marriage is in trouble, and Katie, who's been trying for a baby for a while now.

Lord, you've got good plans for this place, for all of the people here. Lord, please work in this room, send your comfort, your help and your inspiration. Draw all these people closer to you.

I'm going to miss them.

* * * *

July 18th

'Well, I'm sorry. I just think that's a cop-out.'

I'm at cell group and it's just after 9 o'clock. I'd been perilously close to nodding off, but Jack's short response to Lauren makes me sit bolt upright in my seat.

'Thanks for that, Jack. Could you explain exactly what you mean, please?' Lauren's tone is cool, and we all turn to the corner of the room where Jack is perched on a stool.

'Well, it's that phrase you just used: "Preach the gospel at all times; if necessary, use words". A cop-out. It can stop us actually proclaiming the good news to people who need to hear it.'

I notice Ben and Jenny, our cell-group leaders, exchange glances and Jenny says, 'Wasn't that originally said by St Francis of Assisi?'

Jack shrugs. 'Apparently. Some people doubt it. But my main point is that it implies that the gospel should somehow shine through our lives – and the truth of the matter is that most of the time it doesn't. Perhaps we could get away with it if we were as godly as St Francis – and lived accordingly – but I'm nowhere near that level of holiness.'

No one argues with him and he looks slightly disappointed. The room goes silent, and before I know it I've opened my mouth.

'But I think it can shine through people, Jack. You might be surprised who you've influenced. The reason I started coming to this church was because of a lovely couple I knew. They were churchgoers but they never proclaimed the gospel to me. I just wanted to find out more.'

Ben nods. 'Well, it's certainly an interesting debate,' he says. 'But if we never actually say that Jesus is Lord, how is anyone going to find out? Are we just pushing a pale version of Christianity if good deeds are all we have to offer?'

Jack claps his hands. 'Exactly! If we don't proclaim the gospel while helping the poor and sick, aren't we just another social services agency? Sorry, Lauren, am I being unfair?'

Lauren sighs. 'I'm not sure it's as simple as you make out. People get very nervous when they think you're just out to convert them and they get scared off. Sometimes it has to be softly-softly. You can't just start preaching at people and waving the Bible around when they walk through the door. It's about building relationships. A friend of mine ran a toddler group for years at her church, and it was only when the children neared school age and so wouldn't come to the group any more that some of the mums started to ask questions. They realized they were going to miss something – and wondered what it was.'

Jack looks impatient. 'A good illustration of why the gospel should have been explained to them earlier.'

I'm getting rather confused listening to this, and now I'm thinking about my friend Val and her view that most Christians are hypocrites.

I start to talk. 'But hang on a minute. What happens if you *do* proclaim the gospel and don't actually live it out? I mean if you preach the good news and it doesn't make a difference in your life, what kind of advertisement is that for Christianity? People are just going to think it's fake.'

I look around the room. Everyone looks weary and there's a general air of relief when Ben takes charge.

'Well, this is obviously a real challenge for us. But should it be either social justice or preaching? Why can't it be both? We can feed bellies and spirits too.' He pauses. 'How would that work in practice?'

Jenny looks at her watch. 'It's getting late. Let's pray about it and ask God to help us get the right balance. Ruth, why don't you start us off?'

I do my best, but I'm happy when it's time to go. And as I'm walking home with my husband, he looks at me and grins, 'Do you realize that you were actually arguing against yourself in there?'

I grab his hand and smile. It's a clear, cool night, and as I gaze up at the stars I wonder why we have to make being a Christian so very complicated.

Or is it just me?

* * * *

August 1st

I'm at my own leaving do, and have just been chatting with one of Patricia's friends, Tom, a well-known TV reporter from a rival channel. It was all quite pleasant, until I mentioned I went to church.

'Oh,' he said. 'You're one of those. Well, nice to talk to you, but you won't want to spend any more time with me. I'm a second-class citizen in your eyes, not good enough for your churches, and certainly not good enough to have equal rights when it comes to who I share my bed, or even my life, with.'

And off he walked, leaving me standing there, clutching my lemonade and feeling pretty stupid. And cross. I don't care if he's gay!

What is going on here? What this man is, and what he's not, is nothing to do with me, surely? How has it come to this, that Christians are only known for what we're supposedly against?

I consider running after Tom, but that would really be daft. And then I think back to cell group last week when 'Headline Phil' read out that verse about God using the foolish things of the world to shame the wise. He also quoted John Wimber, who said 'I'm a fool for Christ; whose fool are you?'

At that moment Tom turns round and glares at me. I blurt out, 'I don't believe that!' a little too loudly. Some of my colleagues stare as Tom slowly walks back across the room. 'You don't believe what, Ruth?' he barks. 'What don't you believe?'

I look him straight in the eyes. 'I don't believe you're a second-class citizen. That's a ridiculous thing to say.'

'Oh, is it really? So who did I see on the news last week talking about how God hates fags? Protesting at funerals? That's all fine, is it?'

'Oh, please,' I almost laugh. 'No one takes those crazies seriously, do they?'

'Well, actually, that's entirely my point. Yes, they do – it's often the crazies that grab the news headlines. And if you're going to tell me you're a moderate or progressive Christian, then forget it. You stand on the same platform as these people. I don't see many Christians sticking up for us and saying, don't oppress gay people, women, Muslims or whoever these ghastly people are targeting. I never hear about that.'

I'm getting angry now. 'Well, actually, there are a lot of people who would be willing to do that, but often they don't get invited anywhere near a television studio. And that's because we in the media often find it a lot more interesting to broadcast the crazies. A bit of shock and awe, conflict; you can't deny that's what producers are looking for, Tom? When Elton John had a baby with his partner, your channel gave a platform to one of the most outrageous right-wing, anti-gay voices. Fewer than two hundred members of his organization worldwide, but he claimed to speak for Christians everywhere. Was there no one else you could find? Really?'

Tom smiles. 'Well, now I am confused. I know what you're saying, but you can't really turn it round on me. You say you don't want to discriminate, but what do you really believe, Ruth? What do you really think the Bible says?'

I start to talk, but realize it doesn't matter what I say, it's going to sound weak. From the look of his face, Tom has made his mind up. I lost his respect from the moment I told him I was a Christian.

It's a relief when Patricia comes up and changes the subject. And I make my excuses and head off to the toilets.

I look at myself in the mirror. Next week I'll be a 'stay at home mum' and will no longer have any influence in the media. Not that I had much in the first place. I'm not sure I've made any difference at all – at least as far as general perceptions of church are concerned.

More importantly, did Mr Angry back there have a point? By not speaking up, am I allowing people with extreme views to go unchallenged? Does it even matter how churchgoers are seen?

Christians have a strange love/hate relationship with the news. There's a lot of complaining about the media, but there's an awful lot of excitement if someone representing church manages to bag a TV or radio interview.

On the other hand, I've seen some funny attitudes to self-publicity – when someone's in the public eye and is successful it's sometimes almost sneered at, as if they're not showing enough 'Christian' humility. I've read online comments claiming that a very media-friendly bishop was actually attention seeking, that he wanted to further his own agenda. As far as I could see, he was just trying to preach the gospel to as wide an audience as possible.

Well, it isn't my problem any more. I'm tired now. I want to be at home on the sofa. And it suddenly strikes me how easy it would be to just live in a 'Christian' bubble, a ghetto insulated from the big wide world. And after tonight's experience, how tempting.

****

September 13th

'Well, there are things that I find difficult to believe, and there are some things I'm never going to accept.'

Our friends Dave and Jo are round for dinner and we're telling them about some strange 'church' stuff we've heard about. I'm starting to get upset and I don't really know why.

Jo looks at me. 'Why is it bothering you so much?'

I frown. 'It's all just a little bit *too* weird. Gold glitter, white feathers and jewels falling from the sky during worship? People getting "gold teeth"? Why on earth would God do that? What would be the point? Isn't Jesus enough for some people? But most of all, what does all of this look like to non-believers?'

I'm getting a bit carried away, but I'm pretty sure I'm safe here. My husband and I have known Dave and Jo for years, and they are definitely 'feet firmly on the ground' kind of people.

'Oh dear, this has really got to you, hasn't it?' Jo laughs. 'But why has this come up now? It's very interesting, but I don't think it's new.'

'We were talking about it at cell group last week,' James says. 'Some friends told us about a couple they knew who had set up a new church. It was tough going at first, but they really prayed for God's presence, and one Sunday he showed up pretty powerfully. And one thing that happened was that gold dust fell on the pastor's wife's hands.'

'Apparently,' I say, and James shoots me a 'look'.

'If it did happen,' he says, 'it must have really touched her that God had blessed her like that.'

I sigh. James is a lot more open to all this than I am.

'OK, but why does this weird stuff always happen to "Sam at cell group's best friend's cousin", and never to anyone I know personally and trust so I can see for myself whether it's a kind of modern myth? I don't believe anyone's actually making things up maliciously, but these tales can get exaggerated . . .' I stop and look at my friends. There's something going on between them but I'm not sure what. Dave especially is looking a bit, well, shifty.

'What's going on, Dave?' I ask.

'Well, it's just that I can really understand where you're coming from. I used to feel exactly like you . . .'

I don't believe this. 'Used to?'

'Shall we tell them, Jo?'

'I think we'll have to, now.'

'OK. Well, it was eight years ago, and we were going through quite a difficult time. And I was taken along to a "prophetic revival" meeting. I was very cynical and grumpy and sat right at the back. The leaders were praying for people at the meeting to be given gold fillings and for gold dust to fall. And I really didn't think anything of it until the next day when I was drinking coffee and my mouth felt really strange . . .' He pauses and grins at me.

'No, please don't tell me you had one.'

He nods. 'I think God has got an excellent sense of humour. Would you like to see it?'

I look over at my husband who has his head in his hands. Are they all teasing me?

But as Dave opens his mouth I can hardly miss it. A big filling, and it's – gold!

'I don't claim to fully understand it,' he says. 'But Jesus turned water into wine on the third day of the wedding pretty much just to show his glory and deepen his disciples' faith and belief.'

Almost as soon as our friends leave, I start to charge around the kitchen, ranting as I go, 'Right, so I'm not allowed to think that anything is weird any more? I obviously have to accept all this craziness? I've come to church, I've accepted the general message, can just about live with the prophetic 'words' and healings, and I even give them a go myself sometimes. I raise my hand in worship; I pray for people and lay hands on them, and now I've got to believe that God zaps people with gold teeth just to prove his glory! What's going on?'

My husband looks at me sympathetically and I'm suddenly close to tears.

Whatever's next?

* * * *

September 20th

'You know what, James? I know I've been here before, but I'm beginning to think church might just be a bit too weird.' I take a large sip of my gin and tonic and sigh.

It's our wedding anniversary and still warm enough for us to enjoy a drink outside our favourite restaurant.

James laughs, 'Are you still upset about the teeth thing? Or was it the spiritual gift questionnaire at cell group last week? Who would have thought you're actually a worship leader in disguise?'

'Well, there is all that,' I say, 'but today I was flicking through a celeb magazine at Anita's coffee morning when she pointed to a well-known actor and declared that he'd been "washed". Then everyone else chipped in with other famous names and a debate started as to whether they were "washed" too. I had to ask what on earth they were talking about, and was politely informed they meant "washed in the blood of the Lamb". Obviously.'

'The Lamb being . . .'

'Jesus. Yes.'

I look at the drink in my hand – a treat for a pregnant woman on a special occasion.

'Don't get me wrong,' I say. 'The church ladies are all lovely. It's just that I still wonder if I'm more "at home" sitting on a bar stool with a G and T in one hand and cigarette in the other.'

James looks concerned, 'A cigarette? You're joking, aren't you? It took you ages to give them up.'

My husband has never smoked a cigarette in his life. I suddenly picture James as he was nearly twenty years ago, a young, fervent Christian. And I remember opening a Valentine card just after my 21st birthday, comparing the handwriting and realizing it was from him.

I wasn't interested. There was no way on earth I would go out with a serious Christian whose first commitment was church, and who had strong ideas about what was right and what was wrong.

We stayed friends for years, though. He started to mention church less and less, then I started working for the tabloid newspaper and we began to drift apart.

Val tells me James would always ask after me, but that she never dared tell him the full story, that I was drinking myself into a hole on a regular basis and how worried she was. Another memory hits, this time of me with a hangover from hell, scrabbling around in my handbag and finding receipts for places I couldn't even remember going to the night before.

I look over at James. He doesn't really believe I could miss all of that, does he? I think about some of my old colleagues and friends from those days. Several were implicated in the phone hacking scandal. At least two died of alcohol and drugs dependency; others embraced yoga and clean living, and one particularly bad case now writes thrillers and consults the ancient philosophers on how to live a good life.

I wonder what they'd think of me now. Tabloid hack turned born-again Christian. Predictable? Pathetic?

Not that I have a particularly dramatic story to tell. There was no lightning flash conversion for me. I didn't 'give my life to Jesus', and wake up the next morning with no desire to drink and smoke, full of hope and joy.

The change in my life was a very slow and drawn out process: the prayer in the church and then the new job away from the sleaze and stress of the newspaper. A few years went by when nothing much seemed to happen at all. Then, a few months before I was due to move to Africa to work for a charity, I saw James again at Val's birthday party. I remember him asking me to dance, and then laughing so much with this handsome, kind man. I never did get on that plane.

111

My husband's right; it was a long, hard struggle to give up smoking. I still do drink, but I'm always careful. And it was me who dragged us both back to church when I realized I'd been given something precious, and left to my own devices I was going to mess it up.

It's getting cold now and I suddenly feel very tired. I take my husband's hand and smile. 'You mean the world to me, you do know that, don't you? Come on, let's go inside.'

* * * *

October 8th

It's Thursday evening and Ann the Alpha course leader and her husband Colin are round for dinner. My culinary skills have improved in the last year or so, and I'm pleased they seem to be enjoying my chilli.

'I hope you don't mind me bringing this up,' Ann says, 'but I was saying to Colin the other day that I cannot see you as a tabloid reporter. You just look too – well, *nice*. And what I mean is that you are nice too!'

I laugh. 'You'd better ask James about that.'

'Seriously though,' Colin says. 'We just can't imagine you working there.'

I think for a minute. It's not really as if I've undergone a personality transplant since becoming a Christian. 'Well, actually that was partly why I did quite well there,' I say, 'I *was* nice. If you're the editor of a tabloid newspaper, what you don't want are reporters who look like sleazebags. Well, you do want a few of them, but mainly what you want are journalists who are going to get the story; people who you would invite into your front room and pour your heart out to. I'm not saying that we were angels running around heroically exposing wrongdoing. Clearly we weren't, but these days when people imagine a red-top reporter they think of a monster. It's not as simple as that. As for chequebook journalism, the story didn't always go to the highest bidder when I was around; people trusted me and didn't think I was going to stitch them up. And I never deliberately set out to hurt anyone or misrepresent them; it just sometimes seemed to happen. It was just the way the whole thing worked.'

Ann looks confused. 'But you must have been ruthless and really hard to carry on working in that environment.'

'I was.'

James cuts in. 'Not before you worked there you weren't.'

'But James, I must have had some of "that" in me. Although I really, really felt for the people I talked to, people touched by some terrible tragedy, I was always able to detach myself.'

Ann nods. 'But so can doctors, and ambulance and fire crews.'

'Yes, but they're trying to help people. In my first week as a local newspaper reporter I was sent to knock on the door of a little boy who had died of meningitis. When I went there it turned out they'd had the funeral that afternoon. The mum wanted to talk to me; she wanted to talk about her boy. I cried with her.' I stop, and take a deep breath. This is not easy for me to admit. 'But even then I realized that the interview would make a great story, that I might even get the front page. I think I told myself I was working towards some noble end, that it was OK to report someone's private grief and pain, somehow, maybe for the good of humanity. Was I just kidding myself? I know I wrote a lot that helped people, and towards the end of my time at the tabloid I did do some campaigns and important stories, but I'm not sure my motives were ever that straightforward.'

Ann stops me. 'But you told me that at some point when you were working for the tabloid you started to pray for the situations you were coming across. Can you tell us about that?'

I sit back. 'Well, yes. If I was covering an ongoing story I always prayed for the people involved. Babies who had been snatched, hostage situations, disasters. But I remember very strongly a few months before I left the tabloid I was sent to the south coast where two young girls had gone missing on their way to school. It looked as if they'd been abducted, and as I covered press conferences and interviewed friends of the family, I prayed and prayed they would be found quickly and unharmed.

'I was on my own in the hotel one night, and I fell face down on the floor and cried out to God for the little girls, for those poor, poor parents. The next day the girls were found safe and sound. And we went to the beach so the press pack could take photos of them reunited with their parents, a sort of thank you to everyone who had helped look for them. And of course the media had played a huge part in that.

'Then as night fell, some reporters and photographers gathered in the little cul-de-sac where one of the girls lived. She waved out of the window at us in her pyjamas. Perhaps I imagined it, but I could have sworn I saw a shooting star in the sky above her house. I went back to my car, filed my story to the newsdesk, then put my head in my hands and sobbed. I thought about all the people who must have been praying, and what exactly I'd been praying to, if there really was a God.'

'And eventually you ended up with us on the Alpha course,' Ann says. 'Do you know anything about tapestry, Ruth?'

I look at James and laugh. 'No craft's not exactly my strong point. Why do you ask?'

'I ask because if I showed you the back of any tapestry piece it looks a total mess; thread everywhere, chaos. And of course if you turn it over there's a perfect picture. I think sometimes what we see is the messy thread side; that's what it looks like to us, we can't see how God has been working to make something beautiful. You can't always make sense of your past, but I believe God always works for good.'

I nod my head slowly. Last week Uncle Dave tried to explain the Holy Spirit to me, and he made sense when he said it's been described as similar to the Force in *Star Wars*.

Well, the Force is definitely strong in Ann. She's just managed to show me how I might finally begin to find peace with my past.

The conversation around the table has moved on now to last Sunday's sermon and I think back to those evenings on the Alpha course, the enjoyable debates, Ann's talks, and the prayers. God seemed so close. I have never had so many coincidences happen, so many strange experiences as I did in those few months. Oh, and the food they served – delicious! Most evenings every word Ann said seemed to hit home with almost a physical intensity. I would be thinking about something and, lo and behold, the subject would come up at Alpha that evening. I was praying so hard – every lunch break would be spent walking along the river or in the park, chatting to the God I so wanted to trust.

But now, if I look at it square on, I still have the same old questions and doubts that I've ever had. The Old Testament remains a huge problem for me. Yes, Daniel was saved. But the wives and children of the people who accused him were fed to the lions – what's that all about? I've been online and seen all the debates and it still doesn't help.

Having Ann and Colin here makes me realize how much I miss the security and reassurance that being on the Alpha course gave me. I wish I could have somehow bottled that mystery, that feeling of something happening, that spring was coming. In a way I don't want to explain it or rationalize it.

But I live in the real world. My friends who don't believe are in the real world. And tomorrow I'll be back there again.

* * * *

October 20th

'So the first question we'd like you to think about is "When did you first meet Jesus?"'

116

I'm sitting around a table with my husband and several other people who are going to be baptized in a few weeks' time.

We're all being invited to give our testimony on the big day, and this session is meant to help us focus and prepare – so we don't all ramble on for half an hour, I guess.

Most people have started scribbling away but I'm a bit stuck. I've been a Christian for a while now, but right from the start when people started talking about hearing from God or having a 'relationship' with Jesus, I wondered what on earth they meant. And I've never quite worked it out. True, I do pray a lot more than I used to, and often wander around chatting in my head to Jesus. But sometimes it seems a bit one-sided. How am I supposed to hear from him? And when I think I do, why is it all so infuriatingly subtle?

A passage in the Bible that *could* be an answer to prayer. But equally it could be a complete coincidence; had I turned the page I might have read something entirely different.

I've found that the more I look for God and try to 'tune in', the more these 'coincidences' happen. But I still wonder what would have happened if I'd turned another corner, gone into a different shop or left the house five seconds later.

'You're looking puzzled, Ruth.' Martin, one of our elders, pulls up a seat next to me.

'Yes. I'm sorry. It's just that I always feel uncomfortable when people start talking about Jesus in a very personal way. A lot of Christians I know seem to hear from God all the time; they seem to be on his wavelength, if you know what I mean; they find it easy to work him out. But it's never been like that for me, and I'm not sure I really relate to Jesus like that.'

Martin nods. 'How does it work for you, then?'

I pause for a second. 'Sometimes it's almost like a game of Hide and Seek. Answers turn up when I least expect them, when I'm not looking for them or have almost given up. And when I'm praying for people, it's always the things that I nearly *don't* mention that turn out to be the most significant for the person I'm with. Or it's the day that I'm feeling rubbish and really don't want to worship that I end up feeling closest to Jesus . . . that scares me sometimes.' I sigh. 'I'm tying myself up in knots again. I know I'm sounding negative, but I do really want to get baptized. When I look back I know that it's real. Jesus has changed my life and he's changed me and I can never get away from that.'

'Well, that's great,' Martin says. 'Why don't you just tell us that?'

I sit back and think about my past. I remember the first thing God gave me after I cried out to him was a feeling of peace, a sense of well-being – that somehow everything was going to be OK.

Last Sunday our pastor quoted from the 'Dayenu' – a Passover song that celebrates how freedom from slavery was just the start for the Jews; that God just kept piling on more blessings. He'd read out the first line, 'If he had just brought us out of Egypt – it would have been enough.'

I look across the table at my husband, and think of my son and the baby that's growing inside me. Ten years ago, I'd never have dreamt I could be this happy. And suddenly it hits me hard. Lord, you rescued me from the mess I was in, and that would have been enough. Your peace, your comfort; even an ounce of your presence – that would have been enough. But you just keep blessing me, and I have never done anything to deserve it and never will. And I am so grateful.

Lord, I'm getting baptized because I want to make a public statement that I belong to you, whatever is going on in my mind, and whether I feel close to you or not.

For now that's enough.

* * * *

October 31st

I'm at cell group and I'm really quite angry. Someone has just mentioned the television evangelist Pat Robertson.

Soon everyone is talking about what he said about the people of Haiti – the day after an earthquake devastated their country.

I don't even try to hold back. 'What a stupid, stupid thing to say. The Haitians made a pact with the devil? OK, so he didn't actually say that was the reason the earthquake happened, but he might as well have done. And he's not naïve – he must have known what the result of his words would be. Does he even realize the harm he's done? There are Christians all over the world just trying hard to be Jesus to people and – '

'Ruth, it's the Holy Spirit who does the work, not us.' Jenny is gentle as ever.

'But aren't we supposed to be Christ's representatives? And sometimes we don't do a very good job, do we? People think we're irrelevant, ridiculous even; they don't get what Jesus is all about. And when we do just seem to be making some headway, someone like Pat flaming Robertson comes along and messes it all up again – here we go, the judgemental God.'

Some people start to protest and I hold my hands up. 'OK, that was too harsh. But how many thousands of people around the world must have heard what he said and just thought that Christians are the precise opposite of what we're supposed to be . . . what Jesus was – I mean *is* – I don't know what I mean any more. Did you see the pictures coming out of Haiti? The mothers, weeping? How could that be some kind of weird judgement from God?'

I'm nearly crying now, and Jenny steps in. 'We're all upset by this – we're all emotionally overtaken and drained. But Ruth, the Lord reigns and the Lord wins.' She stops for a moment and looks at me. 'Has someone been giving you a hard time about Pat Robertson?'

I almost groan. 'Yes. I had my friend Val on the phone the other day. She brought up what he said, and there's no way I can throw platitudes at her, she's straight on the Internet checking out all the theological websites. She started talking about Moses and God and the plagues and the Egyptian children who died, saying that the God of the Bible is vengeful and judgemental, just like Pat Robertson said, and I didn't have a clue what to say to her. I ask myself similar questions all the time. I was going to invite her to our baptisms on Sunday but I don't have the heart to now.'

Jenny nods. 'Well, I think you should still invite her. She's certainly got God in her sights, hasn't she?'

I start to smile. I've never looked at it that way before.

Jenny's husband, Ben, is approaching with his laptop. 'Who knows what was in Pat Robertson's head when he said what he did, and what he was trying to say. I prefer the Archbishop of York's take on things.' He points to his computer and reads, 'When the disaster happened, Dr Sentamu said, "I have nothing to say that makes sense of this horror – all I know is that the message of the death and resurrection of Jesus is that he is with us."'

As Ben folds down the laptop my phone starts to buzz in my handbag and I scramble for it, in case it's the babysitter. But it's not. It's Val, and her voice sounds rather odd.

'Ruth . . .' Something's up. 'Val, what's wrong?'

'It's Mum. She's collapsed. I'm on my way to the hospital now. Ruth . . .' The phone goes silent for a moment. 'Ruth . . . Will you pray for her?'

For a moment I'm speechless, but then I get a grip. 'Val, I'm at cell group. We'll all pray now – when I get off the phone, I mean, if you're OK with that.'

'Yes. Thanks.'

'I'll call you tomorrow, unless I hear from you first.'

A thirty-second phone conversation and the world's a very different place.

I look up at ten concerned faces. 'My friend Val needs to know that God is with her. Can we pray?'

* * * *

November 4th

I've just been baptized in a big pool at the front of our church. Jenny is handing me a big fluffy towel and I feel elated.

'So how was it?' she asks.

I pause for a moment and look around at the three hundred or so worshippers in the room.

'Well, giving my testimony was quite scary. Everyone looked so serious; it was like a sea of blank faces. I felt like saying, "Someone *do* something – nod, smile!" And then when someone did look at me in a sympathetic way, I nearly cried. After that I started to look at the clock. It was safer.'

Jenny smiles and we turn and watch the last baptism of the morning. Just before I pick up my bag to get changed she says, 'I liked what you said about what baptism means to you – about drawing a line under the past and trusting your future to God, whatever happens. You've got a very childlike faith.'

I nod wisely, but as I walk away I wonder exactly what that means. Is a childlike faith a bad thing? Should I be striving for a more grown-up, intellectual version of Christianity?

Maybe I should start to think more about what I believe and why. I have to admit that when people argue about subjects such as predestination or the exact meaning of the cross, I start to drift off.

Christians do seem to have very strong views on what is the right thing – or the wrong thing – to believe.

Take the atonement, for example – a theological hot topic, but the whole thing bemuses me. Everyone thinks they are right, even if they have very different views. They've all studied the Bible and put it in the right context, and are confident that they have the correct balance between justice and mercy.

Hmmm. Perhaps I'm better off with a simple faith.

I'm in the toilet sorting out my wet clothes when Hazel, one of our elders, comes in.

She gives me a hug and asks how I'm feeling.

'Actually at this precise moment I'm wondering whether I should be trying to work out exactly why Jesus had to die, and think a bit more about where I stand on certain things.'

'Well,' she laughs, 'I wasn't expecting you to say that. But you know what C.S. Lewis said about the cross – that the theories behind it are not as important as the thing itself, and that we should leave them alone if they don't help us. Personally I'm happy to live with the mystery.'

So am I. And as I walk back towards the main hall, the words of one of my favourite songs drift down the corridor: 'Age to age, He stands, And time is in His hands . . . '

I don't really like thinking about time, and God being outside it.

If God really does have the beginning and the end of the world in his hands, then we really don't have a clue about anything. How can we?

When you think about it like that, a childlike faith is really the only kind of faith you can have.

I reach the back of the hall, and join the singing: 'Name above all names . . . '[1]

Words such as *reverence, fear, holy,* and *glory* all seem to make more sense to me when I think about eternity and how immense and awesome God must be.

123

And yet, he says we are his children.

Suddenly the band stops playing and we're all singing unaccompanied. It's almost eerie in its beauty.

Normally I get completely lost in corporate worship and love being part of a bigger thing. But now I can hear myself singing. I listen to my voice and I realize I sound like a little girl. A little girl who has just stood up in front of this church and committed her future to God.

I smile as I look around the room and think maybe that's all any of us are – just little children reaching for our Father's hand.

* * * *

Tuesday, 2 p.m.

Dear Dad,

I've been thinking about eternity again, and it's not good. It says in the Bible that God has put eternity in our hearts. Well, sometimes I wish he hadn't.

Actually, the rest of the Bible quote says we can't fathom what God has done from beginning to end. That pretty much sums it up. As James said, our brains are just not wired to understand it. And that's fair enough. God is God and we are his children.

But then I think back to Noah again, and the whole redemption story. The argument that many Christians use is that when he saw things were going wrong, God was actually very kind, and instead of wiping us all out and starting again, he saved Noah, and that the pattern was repeated – time after time we turned our back on God until Jesus was the final solution. I get all that, and I understand that God gave us free will so we could make our own choices.

But free will or not, if God is outside time, surely he knew when the world was created that we would rebel against him – actually he must have known what the end result would be before he even began. *That's utterly mind-boggling, yet most Christians seem to happily ignore it.*

And I still want to know, if God is outside of time, what does he do with his – er – time, but again that's missing the point.

I read somewhere that some people have tried to get round the 'time' question by suggesting that God might deliberately close his mind to the future.

At this stage the hard drive in my brain starts to give off steam and my head starts spinning like that unfortunate girl in The Exorcist *(yes, Dad, you banned me from watching it but I still did).*

Is this the kind of stuff they talk about at theological college? I think I'd go slightly mental, debating unanswerable questions.

In fact I think the best thing for me at the moment is to go and make myself a hot chocolate.

I'm starting to think the only way through this is to take that leap of faith and believe that God is good, and that Jesus rescues us. And that when he declared you have to enter the kingdom as a child, it was one of the most important things he ever said.

Thursday, 8 p.m.

I'm in the process of learning a new game. It's called biblical ping-pong and it seems to be quite popular among Christians of all denominations and persuasions. It goes like this: Firstly, you state what you believe to be a fact. For example: 'Dogs don't go to heaven.' Then your opponent says, 'Aha, but wait' and quotes a Bible verse at you. You then respond with a Bible verse that backs up your argument, and so on and so on, until someone gets upset or everyone gives up and goes home (or logs off).

Oh, and the most important part of this game is that you have to believe that you are right and everyone else is wrong.

I have witnessed this several times, both online and in person, and am often tempted to join in and offer an opinion – and then not quote a Bible verse at all, just to unite them against one common unbiblical, heathen enemy.

It's not that I don't believe in the Bible. I really want to. It's just that sometimes it's brandished as a weapon and I don't think that's the point at all.

I'm well aware there are lots of interesting and good-natured theological debates happening in cyberspace and in person, and that it's important to thrash out this stuff.

But when I'm party to a debate where people aren't listening to each other, and just want to prove their own point, it actually makes me wary of the Bible. When I start to think of all the different ways it's been interpreted, I feel slightly sick, as if something I thought made sense to me means something else entirely.

The row over what exactly was achieved on the cross happened when I first came to church as an adult, and the fallout was bewildering to me as a new Christian. I've heard variations of that debate several times since, over issues such as women in leadership, and sexuality – people with wildly differing views quoting from the text, saying, 'I'm right and this is the way to see things.'

I don't have any theological training. I'm not likely to get any, either. And I don't have the time for serious study; twenty minutes' reading at bedtime is the most I can manage at the moment.

I'm just a person in the pews, a run-of-the mill believer. I thought Jesus came for ordinary people like me, and he gave the very well-educated Pharisees and Sadducees a bit of stick for tying people up in knots.

I really do want to learn more. I want insight and wisdom, and I don't want to remain uneducated. But sometimes the debates depress me so much I don't want to pick up the Bible at all.

Thursday, 2 p.m.

I think I'm going to cry; I'm so frustrated. I've just had two chats with friends about the church, and I can't believe what I heard.

The first conversation happened with Janet's husband in their kitchen. I'd asked him what he thought about his visit to our church for Daniel's dedication back in May.

It was very interesting, he said, but he could never go to church because the whole thing's a joke.

I was expecting him to say something about the 'weird' healing stuff at the end, but no. 'It's just the way Christians go on,' he said, 'arguing with each other all the time; people are fed up with hearing about the latest splits; we just don't care.' And just for good measure, he added, how would he know what to believe anyway? Everyone seems to have a different idea on what the Bible says or exactly what Jesus meant.

Marie, from work, has actually been going to church, but she's not happy either. Apparently at her church there are two kinds of Christian – 'proper Christians, and second-class ones'.

At the 9 a.m. service you get all the mums from school, and it's 'quite relaxed and nice' and then there are the 'really serious Christians' who go to the 10.30 a.m. service.

'I get the impression that they don't think we're proper Christians at all,' she told me. 'I once went to the evening service. It was very cold outside, but as soon as I entered church I was hissed at to remove my hat, and that pretty much sums up the way we're treated. I've started to read the Bible, but I don't agree with everything that I hear. That's not a problem for me at all. I want my son to go to a good school and I want him to be taught the Bible stories and I am interested; but I'm not going to start changing my opinions to match theirs. If people have an issue with that, then it's their lookout really.'

Dad, I don't want to church-bash. I've been told the church is the Bride of Christ and that I mustn't criticize or be negative, but this is happening in the real world. This is what some people outside of church think about what is going on inside. And I do think we should be concerned how others see us. As Christians, we bear the name of Christ and we should be glorifying him.

Sunday, 7 p.m.

I'm glad I do go to church. I'm glad there are so many people there who are much wiser and more learned than me!

This morning our pastor quoted from Mere Christianity *by C.S. Lewis. Apparently Lewis thought Christianity is like a house with many rooms and a big hall. The rooms represent different churches and denominations, and the idea is for people to leave the hall and enter one of the rooms where there are fires and chairs and meals.*

Lewis said you must choose your door carefully and then be kind to people who have chosen the other rooms, because we are all living in the same house – with Jesus the thing we have in common, I assume?

I wonder what Lewis would think about Christianity at the moment. An unruly house, perhaps, with people running into each other's rooms, criticizing the décor, and putting the faithful off their meals? Or, more importantly, putting outsiders off coming into the hall in the first place?

I realize I'm being harsh. And maybe my friends are using bad experiences as an excuse because they just don't want to know. But I want them to see what I've seen, the good things, the friends we've made, the lives changed. At church this morning there was a call to give your life to Christ, and two young men who'd been going to an outreach group literally ran to the front. We all cheered. Nothing deterred them; they heard the message and responded. And I know that it's not a fairy tale ending, Dad; I know from my own experience that it's just the start of their journey. But our pastor said that God will be found by those who seek him, and Amen to that. I'm so tired of the rows and the controversies and the issues and the stances.

Sometimes I just want to walk away but I can't and I won't. I've promised, you see; I've made a commitment to God that whatever happens, I will see this through.

At the dedication, our pastor said that God's love, peace, joy and forgiveness are to be experienced, not just to be believed or discussed.

That made sense to me. I want more of that. Can that be the next stage, do you think?

> *Your loving daughter,*
> *Ruth*

PART SIX:

THE LORD REIGNS

November 20th

It's Saturday afternoon, and I'm standing outside a makeshift tent in our high street feeling a strange mixture of excitement and fear.

Somehow I agreed to take part in a cross-church project to minister at our town's winter festival. The idea is to approach people on the street, lead them into the tent and pray for them. It sounds simple, but now I'm here I'm panicking. There's a sick feeling in my stomach and I'm actually starting to shake.

What was I thinking of? I have absolutely no problem praying for complete strangers, but this is the town where I grew up. I *know* people here. They're going to think I'm . . . what . . . weird? Odd?

Why would I care? I never thought I was embarrassed about my faith – though clearly I am. I'm wearing a baseball cap, sunglasses, and am now standing behind a tree. But I haven't got time to analyze my feelings. All I know is that this would be a whole lot easier if it was taking place in the bigger town a couple of miles down the road.

Sooner or later I'm going to be recognized. And sure enough, as I look up, a friend of my parents is walking towards me.

'Ruth! How are you doing?' We talk for a few minutes, and though she seems to be deliberately ignoring the fact I'm wearing a big yellow sticker that says, 'Prayer Team', we're having a nice chat.

I suddenly feel bold. Perhaps this is going to be easier than I thought. So I take a deep breath and hear myself say, 'Would you like to come into our prayer tent? No pressure, but if there's anything in your life that you'd like prayer for, then I'd be happy to . . . er . . . fire off a couple of missives, as if were.'

'No thanks,' she says simply, peering into the tent as if there's something nasty inside. And off she walks.

I feel almost indignant. I was only offering to pray, not trying to sell her life insurance. Surely she can't think everything is perfect in her world?

I look up and down the high street and think again that a lot of the people in this town, and the people in this country, have got it quite easy. Maybe they don't need to believe; they don't have any major issues. Their lives are fine, thank you very much.

Did Jesus come for people with nice ordered lives?

It wasn't like that for me. I knew that I couldn't make it on my own; that I needed God in my life.

I think of Val and how her attitude has softened since her mum had a stroke and some people from my cell group started to pray for them both.

Encouraged, I head inside the tent, and it's only when I turn round that I realize that someone has followed me in.

It's a good-looking woman in her fifties. She sits down in front of me and says, 'I'd like to pray about my son. I'm a Muslim, by the way.'

'Oh, that's nice.' *Nice?* What am I talking about? 'You know we're Christians? I guess the sign saying "Churches Together" might just give it away.'

'Yes,' she says, and a gentle smile slowly spreads across her face. Does she realize I'm way out of my depth here?

'OK, well, what can I pray for?'

So she tells me, and I start to pray for her and her family. The whole world could be passing by outside the tent, but it's peaceful inside, just the two of us.

And I realize the Holy Spirit has shown up too when she starts to cry and says she feels God is so close to her.

As I walk home later, I start to think about Allah and who that lady was praying to, and whether it matters. But I soon give up. Yet again my assumptions have been challenged. Whenever I think I'm close to working something out, I'm soon forced to think again.

God used me. He did. For some season he used *me* to reach out to that lady, and she was blessed.

I think I'll leave the rest to him.

* * * *

133

December 1st

'Well, I do believe that Jesus was raised from the dead.'

Val pauses to spear a carrot with her fork, and I stare at my husband in disbelief.

I'm desperately trying not to express shock. I can see James is too, because his left eyebrow is raised, which is always a sign.

When we invited Val and her boyfriend, Keno, round for dinner, this was definitely not what we expected.

Certainly her view of the church has softened recently. But she hasn't become a Christian and been 'saved', as my fellow believers would say. I've known for a while now that she believes in God and prays, but this latest revelation is a bit of a bombshell.

'OK, Val, so what exactly does that mean to you?'

'Well it means just that. I believe that Jesus died and then came back to life. I believe we all do.'

James looks excited. 'So does that mean you're going to come to church?'

'No. Am I not allowed to hold an opinion on religion without coming to church? I'll accept that some of the church people I've met recently have been lovely, and I'm really grateful that they've been praying for Mum, but I think I'm still allergic to most Christians.'

I should have known this was never going to be straightforward. Why is it that since I became a follower of Christ, I haven't managed to lead one person to him?

I sigh. 'OK, Val, but based on what you just said about the resurrection, you are practically a Christian.'

'Yes, sure – apart from the thorny and controversial issue of hell.' Hell. But of course.

'You see, I don't believe that hell exists. I think that view puts me at odds with most of your church friends. Am I right? But I just don't believe in it.'

I jump in. 'OK, but what *do* you believe?'

'I think we're all on a kind of celestial conveyor belt and we go up and down to heaven until we've learnt enough to live there. So even someone like Myra Hindley will keep being reincarnated, and maybe she's come back already and this time is learning what it's like to suffer.'

I don't even try to argue, and later as I'm clearing up I wonder exactly what you have to believe to be a Christian.

Obviously Val has some kind of faith in Jesus. She believes in the resurrection, even if she doesn't go to church and thinks there's a heavenly escalator. Does that mean she's not a Christian? And most important of all, what does that mean about her eternal fate?

Actually, when it comes to hell, I have a lot in common with my friend. I don't think I'll ever be able to accept that a loving God would damn people to hell just because they haven't said a personal prayer of acceptance.

Can *I* still be a Christian even if I don't toe the standard, evangelical party line? No one can control what goes on inside my head, but is it OK to privately hold views that might be different to the elders in our church? Or should I start looking for a more 'liberal' church? I know there are all kinds of shades of belief out there.

135

But we're more than happy where we are. I turn to my husband. 'James, why do we believe what we do? We believe what we're told. How do we know what we're told is – well, right?'

He shrugs. 'We have to trust our pastors and their view of things. Most people don't have the time to spend hours researching stuff; even then, doesn't it all depend on what teacher or book you have, which tradition you're coming from?'

Not for the first time I wonder why everything has to be so complicated. But I can't think about this now. We've got dishes to wash and a lively little boy who will be bouncing around in – oh, about five hours' time.

I smile as I think about my son – and wonder again how I'm going to explain my beliefs to him as he gets older. When it comes down to it, my faith should be simple enough for a child to understand.

Shouldn't it?

* * * *

December 8th

It's Saturday morning and I'm in the car with Val. We're heading out for a coffee with Daniel in tow.

I'm tired, not in the best of moods, and we're in a traffic jam. There's an advert on a bus shelter in the high street that makes me growl every time I drive past. Today we're stuck right in front of it.

The poster is trying to sell some kind of baby food, and shows two pristine young mums holding their beautifully well turned out toddlers. According to the ad the women are called Kate and Emma, and they really get on my nerves.

I don't normally feel driven to acts of vandalism, but I have fantasized about sneaking out in the middle of the night with a marker pen and adding a touch of realism in the form of bags under eyes, wild hair and stains on clothes. And maybe a couple of devil's horns for one of the toddlers. Childish, but it cheers me up.

'Look at that.' I wave my arm vaguely. Val's head snaps up like a meerkat's. 'What, where?' she says.

'That. Kate and Emma over there. Look at them. Serene, in control, lovely shiny hair and perfect skin. Look how they're dressed casually but with so much care, and they gaze adoringly at their gorgeous children as they offer a tasty but healthy snack from their fashionable yet practical handbags. Only the best, of course. I hate them.'

'Ruth!' Val feigns shock, and then a wicked grin spreads across her face. 'Actually,' she says, 'I was thinking they look like the very best specimen of evangelical Christians. Just look at those smiles.'

Oh, here we go again. But today I can't be bothered to argue, and actually she has a point. I nod. 'Yes, they could well be A-class Christians. In fact, I bet they both run the crèche, cook wholesome meals for those in need (in the church, and wider community) and lead cell group on a Wednesday night.'

I really have met women like that. I'm definitely not one of them. These days I usually turn up for church looking like I've had a fight with a hedge on the way – and lost.

I'm learning that becoming a mother is quite similar to becoming a Christian. It's a lot tougher than it's often portrayed . . . and somehow you feel you're 'meant' to look joyful and serene when you're often the opposite.

I start to rant. 'Seriously, though, do you remember me telling you about "Biscuit Mum"?'

Val nods slowly.

'Biscuit Mum' made a strong impression on me. She was sitting opposite as I waited to see a midwife for an antenatal check. She had a newborn baby and toddler in tow, and was not exactly a great advert for motherhood. She looked beyond tired, her skin was grey, but what struck me most of all was the fact that she was literally covered in biscuit crumbs and didn't seem to care, or even be aware of the fact. In short, she was struggling and I really felt for her.

I turn to Val. 'That's why adverts like that make me cross. Can you imagine someone like that poor lady seeing "Kate and Emma" and wondering where she'd gone wrong? And not just her; I see mums who seem to have it all together, but something's not quite right, and sometimes I wonder what goes on behind closed doors. I've certainly had awful days when I've been so tired and everything is too much, and I've only just made it back into the house after playgroup before bursting into tears. I love Daniel so much, but some mornings I look at the clock, it's only 8 a.m. and I wonder how I'm going to make it through till tea time. There's *so* much pressure to pretend all is well, and of course you need to "have" the right thing. Val, if you ever get pregnant, be careful with the baby magazines, they – '

I stop. Val's not really listening. Daniel has fallen asleep in his car seat and she's gazing at him. But something's wrong; she looks sad.

I start to think. How long has Val been with her boyfriend now? Doesn't she want to have . . . ?

Oh.

The traffic starts moving and I feel like banging my head on the dashboard. I'm supposed to be her best friend. Why am I such a fool?

* * * *

December 11th

It's Sunday morning, I'm standing in church and I'm really struggling. My mind keeps wandering back to yesterday evening – and what happened when I popped out for a pint of milk.

Just as I was leaving the shop, I walked straight into a lady who used to go to our church. A few years ago, she lost her grown-up daughter to cancer and I hadn't seen her for a while. I'd just assumed she'd found another church, so when I asked where she was going now I was thrown by her reply.

'I don't go any more.'

'To church? Oh.' I didn't even think. 'Why?' would have been an obvious question, but I thought I knew the answer.

'Because of what happened to Emily?'

She sighed and looked up at the sky. 'Yes, in a way. The church puts so much emphasis on healing these days it's difficult for those of us who haven't seen that happen. Emily prayed so hard for a miracle. We all did. And then nothing happened.'

'But she had such an amazing faith in Jesus. I remember going for a coffee with her a couple of months after I started coming to church. She was so strong.'

The woman's voice shook as she spoke. 'At the end it didn't seem to help her. She was scared. She didn't want to die. I just can't believe it's as simple as it's all made out to be, and I don't feel there's a place for me at church any more. And what I do know is that I just can't deal with it now.'

As she walked off I felt like I'd said all the wrong things, even though there were no right things to say.

Now I'm standing in church looking around, feeling helpless. People here do believe in healings and miracles and I still don't know what to make of it all.

I've prayed for people with mild ailments and they've reported an improvement, sometimes, I suspect, just to encourage me. And I've prayed for people to have babies . . .

Just as I'm thinking that, my eyes rest on Keira, across the aisle from me. She's been trying for a baby for some years now. I've been praying for her and her husband. The whole church has been praying for them. Recently I've almost been shouting at God – please just give them a baby, Lord, *please*. I look down at my own heavily pregnant belly, and suddenly it's all too much.

I inch my way to the end of the aisle – and walk out of church.

I've been heading this way for a while now. I've always had my doubts and questions, but recently they've been buzzing around my head like wasps.

Have I got this all wrong? Have I somehow been swept up in some kind of religious mania and not really thought things through?

I don't know if I believe in miracles. I don't even know if I believe the right things to be a Christian – issues such as heaven, hell and homosexuality just make me confused.

Maybe I should just step back for a while. I mean, I could still pray and believe in God couldn't I? I just wouldn't have to take it all so seriously. What would happen if my husband and I were less *involved* in church? If we dropped our commitments and tithes, we'd have more time and money for a start.

I sit down on the bench outside and imagine one of the elders coming out and having exactly the right words to reassure me. Or maybe Keira will find me, say she's expecting a baby, and ask me to pray for her. But nothing happens, and I remember that woman's face last night as she told me about Emily, and how scared her daughter had been.

I choke back tears and try to keep calm.

I'm obviously having a bad day. Perhaps all I need is to go home and sleep, and I'll wake up back to normal tomorrow.

After all, no one ever said this was going to be easy, and people in the Bible had off-days too, didn't they? Jacob wrestled with God, Peter got it wrong, Thomas doubted and Paul struggled.

Lord, please help me. And I get up, take a deep breath and walk back in.

* * * *

January 8th

We're driving to church on Sunday morning. A car cuts me up, and I start to furiously pound on my horn.

'Ruth, calm down.' James is cross.

'I'm sorry – did you miss that total moron who nearly caused a major accident? How would you prefer I react? Smile sweetly and wave him on?'

'Yes, well, we're on our way to church, remember? Try not to lose it completely before we get there.'

Oh yes. Church. I'm still struggling. I'm out of sorts, grumpy and really wrestling with questions about healings and miracles.

And why shouldn't I beep my horn? Do the fruit of the Spirit still have to come through even when some maniac is putting my family's life at risk?

Do I have to at least try to be nice all the time? Most Christians I've come across are so polite and *positive* about everything. They never seem to say the wrong thing.

Sometimes, though, I do wonder how honest it all is. What would happen if we really said what was on our minds, instead of the 'right' thing?

As we reach church, I look around the car park. There's the woman who often comes up and says, 'I was going to phone you this week' – but never does. And there's the man who sometimes barges in on conversations I was having, as if I wasn't even there. Don't even mention the people who chat right next to the coffee table, causing a massive log jam.

What would happen if, one Sunday morning, I just snapped? I smile as I imagine shouting 'Move along please!' from the back of the drinks' queue. Maybe next time my responses to the people in the car park will be 'Why didn't you call, then?' or 'Excuse me, am I the invisible woman?'

No, it's not going to happen. I should be aspiring to patience, kindness and goodness, not trying to upset people.

I'm queuing for the crèche now and starting to calm down. A couple with a young girl is just ahead of me. They look unsure and explain to the leader that it's their first time at church; they are here for the christening. My cheeks redden. Cripes, I hope it wasn't them I beeped on the way here.

What is the matter with me at the moment? Why am I so touchy? Nothing has changed at church – it must be something to do with me. I wish I could put my finger on what's bothering me so much about healings and miracles. We pray for them a lot at our church and I really do want to believe, but I don't know if I've ever seen a real, proper, cast-iron one. And deep down I think I'm worrying that we're just peddling false hope to people, with the best of intentions of course.

There's one thing I do know. I'm not in a good place at the moment, and I need to get this sorted out before I can move forward.

I try to engage with the service, but I can't seem to concentrate and more than ever I feel like an outsider. At the end I almost groan when our pastor says he feels there are people here today that God wants to heal. He mentions some specific conditions, and I watch as dozens walk up to the front to be prayed for.

Normally, I would help to minister, but today I feel stuck to my seat. Soon, though, everyone is being prayed for . . . but what's going on there? Out of the corner of my eye, I see the couple from the crèche queue walk past me. They are now standing nervously at the side, holding their little girl in their arms.

Our pastor's wife has spotted them, and I start to well up as the scene unfolds before my eyes – the wife crying, the husband explaining, and then the pastor's wife laying her hands on the small child. Something inside me seems to break, and I cry out, 'Please, Lord, please answer their prayer, whatever it is. I want this all to be true; I want to see people get healed. Lord, please show me a miracle.'

* * * *

January 24th

It's the middle of the night and I'm lying in bed with my hands on my tummy. Our baby's due in a few weeks' time, and I'm getting stomach cramps. In fact, they're starting to come every fifteen minutes.

I did pray to God to show me a miracle a few weeks ago. But I didn't mean an everyday miracle like giving birth – I was thinking more spectacular healing, GOD TV-style.

I don't think I've ever really seen one of those before, even though plenty of people at church tell me they've seen legs grow longer, deaf people healed and people jumping out of their wheelchairs.

The last time I went on a serious miracle hunt was several years ago, and I wasn't a Christian.

I snuggle up and try to get comfortable as the memories flood back. I was working at the newspaper at the time. The editor didn't venture out of the office very often and his request completely threw me.

'I want you to find me a miracle, Ruth.'

I managed what I hoped was an enthusiastic smile. 'OK, yes. Where would you like me to start?'

'Here,' he said, and placed a piece of paper on my desk. On it he'd written the name of a strange-sounding church in Essex.

'It's in my hometown,' he said 'and I can't go anywhere at the moment without seeing these massive posters saying "Healing and Miracles". I'd like you to go there and find one, please.'

'Yes – and? What's the real story? Is the vicar up to no good?'

'Not as far as I know. No; no hidden agenda this time. I just want you to find me a bona fide miracle and write about it. Cheer the readers up a bit, eh?'

So I made a call to the church and asked if I could interview someone who'd been healed. They invited me to a service, and a few days later I was off to deepest Essex with a photographer in tow, in search of the supernatural.

It was not the kind of church I remembered from childhood. I was used to pews and pulpits, but this looked more like a conference centre.

There were strange songs, and then men took microphones and shouted a lot. Some people went up to the stage, but nothing miraculous happened as far as I could see.

The photographer and I sat patiently through the service. Nothing anyone said meant anything to me, and we'd just decided to call it a day when a young man asked what we were doing there. I told him, and then, for some reason, asked how long he'd been at the church and why he had started in the first place. I wasn't expecting the reply – that he had started coming not long ago, after his wife died, and that the people from the church had just been so kind. And that he hadn't seen any amazing healings either, but he wouldn't have got through the last few months without the people he'd met there. He'd started to cry, and some of his friends came up and gently led him away. We'd left soon after.

The church eventually sent me some stories of people they said had been healed, but I couldn't get the medical records to satisfy the editor, and in the end the whole thing was quietly dropped. But I couldn't stop thinking about the strange service and the people who'd looked after that young man, and it bothered me.

Years later and I'm still asking, what did I see there? Not the lame walking or the deaf hearing. It was a simple story of kindness and compassion that got to me, and something shifted in my heart.

Lord, I'd still like to see a miracle, though. If that's OK with you.

Another stomach pain hits hard and I wince. The cramps are getting stronger now. I get up and walk into my son's room. I watch him sleeping and then bend down for a moment to stroke his hair.

There's been so much healing in my life since I invited the Lord to come in – so many 'everyday' miracles. I think I'm just about ready for the next one.

I go back to the bedroom and nudge my husband. 'Sweetheart, I think you'd better wake up. The baby's on its way.'

* * * *

February 20th

I'm standing at the front of a church I've never been to before, talking into a microphone while my baby snoozes on my shoulder.

When my husband and I were asked to take part in a 'ministry trip', I hadn't thought it would take place so soon after giving birth. But here we are, along with several people from our cell group, and I'm really trying to give it a go.

We've been praying for this church for a few weeks, and are now in the process of giving out 'words' and 'pictures' to the congregation. In a few minutes we'll help to pray for people.

I'm doing my best but am really not sure what I'm saying, and whether it's coming from the Holy Spirit or my own imagination.

Faith has been a bit of a struggle recently and I've been feeling far from God. But now I'm a mother of a 2-year-old and a baby I don't have the luxury, or the energy, to think too deeply about things. These days I'm mainly running around in a strange half-awake state, and as I hand on the microphone, I hope I've made some kind of sense.

Now it's time for Lucy's feed, so yet again there's no time to worry. I am not going to start analyzing all this again. I'm just not.

When I return, proceedings are coming to a close. It's ministry time and James is praying for a man at the back of the main hall.

I put my baby in her carrycot and scan the room. A group of people are huddled around a young woman who is sobbing. They all look like church regulars – they are clearly looking after her, and I'm just about to walk past when I think of something that might help.

Feeling bold, I walk straight up.

'Hello. Would you mind if I shared a Bible verse with you? It's to do with Matt Redman, I mean one of his songs, not the man himself . . . er, yes – "The Father's Song",[1] do you know it? Hang on a second, I'll look it up.'

The group of people is looking at me very strangely, especially the woman who's being prayed for. Have I said the wrong thing?

Feeling flustered I start to rifle through my Bible – where *is* that verse?

'Oh, I've got it. Here you go. It's Zephaniah 3 verse 17.' I start to read: '"The LORD your God is with you, he is mighty to save. He will take great delight in you, he will quiet you with his love, he will rejoice over you with singing." It inspired Matt Redman to write his song, apparently. The rest of the chapter is quite good, too.'

I look up to a sea of faces still staring at me. It's not the reaction I expected, and I'm just about to walk away when one of the women speaks.

'That's amazing.'

'Is it?' I'm really confused now. Perhaps they have quite low rates of expectation at this church.

'No, I mean that really is amazing. Jane here has been going through a really tough time recently, and just five minutes ago I read the exact same verse out to her.'

'What, Zephaniah?' I'm almost defensive. 'I really didn't hear you. I was in the crèche, feeding my baby.'

'Yes, I saw you come in.' The woman turns back to her friend. 'There you go, Jane. It's the Lord. You can't deny that now, can you?'

No, she can't. And nor can I. Thank you, God. Thank you for blessing this woman with that lovely verse. But I don't think the blessing was just for her.

I just love it when stuff like this happens. And I've missed this feeling. When I was a new Christian it seemed that not a week would go by without an amazing coincidence that obviously wasn't a coincidence at all.

I glance over at the door. My husband has collected our little boy and is waiting patiently. I can't wait to tell him all about it.

I pick up my daughter in her carrycot and go to join the rest of my family. There's a smile on my face – and hope in my heart.

* * * *

April 21st

It's Saturday morning and I'm tidying the front garden and exchanging pleasantries with passing neighbours.

There's been a lot of talk at our church recently about ministering to the people who actually live next door to us, and I wonder how that could work in our little road.

Really though, the people here have pretty much got the good neighbour thing sewn up. I look up and down the road and think of Peggy, the kind lady at number 6, who died recently after a long illness. As she got more and more sick, not a day went by when I didn't see one of them go in to help, check, pick up shopping, or make a meal. I don't know if any of them are Christians. My husband and I reckon we'd have to do something pretty extraordinary to stand out and be 'good witnesses'.

I smile to myself, and when I look up, Anna from number 12 is peering over the wall.

We chat for a few minutes about how our new baby is doing.

'I knew it was going to be a girl,' she announces, and I realize I'm supposed to ask how – so I do.

'Chinese Birth Charts! They've never let me down. Ever since my cousin told me about them, I've been able to predict the sex of imminent babies. Weird, but it works.'

It's becoming clear to me that there are very different kinds of Christians. The very direct Bible-believing type and the more laid-back 'just say a prayer and let the Holy Spirit do the work'.

I think of Uncle Dave – he's very solid and never misses an opportunity to introduce Jesus into a conversation. He certainly wouldn't put up with Chinese Birth Chart nonsense.

But I'm not sure I'm that type of Christian. And it strikes me that I can't just stand here and tell Anna that I think she's wrong. She'd be quite – well . . . *offended*. Some people would say so be it, that the gospel is there to cause offence. I've heard that a lot. I've also been told that maybe I need to push myself a little more and step out of my comfort zone. But I quite like being comfortable, thank you very much.

I smile at Anna. 'That does sound very interesting. But I'm not really into stuff like that.'

'Oh.' She looks disappointed, and we talk for a few more minutes before she walks away.

Great, that just sounded snotty. And have I missed a really good opportunity to share my faith? I sigh. I just want to go to church and worship God and do my best for him. Lord, is that enough?

A few minutes later, I look up. Someone else has come to chat, but this time it's the daughter of the lady who died a few weeks ago. I ask how she's doing and we talk for a while about the funeral, and how she's missing her mum so much.

'She used to call every day at 5 p.m. and I'm starting to hate that time. I just keep expecting her to ring. I look at the phone and when it stays silent I want to throw it at the wall.'

I nod slowly.

'And when the phone does ring, I get so excited – I can't help thinking it's her.' Then she looks straight at me and says, 'Do you think there's a heaven? Do you think my mum will be with my dad now? Do you believe that?'

I don't know if her mum went to church. I don't know if her dad was a believer or if either of them ever said a prayer of acceptance to Jesus. I don't know what I should say – what, as a Bible-believing Christian, I'm *supposed* to say. There's so much I don't know, and never will. But I know that I believe that Jesus was a kind man who said 'love thy neighbour'. As I'm speaking I pray for peace for the woman standing in front of me.

'Yes. I do believe that. I do really believe that your mum is in heaven with your dad.'

And as she walks away I pray that it's true.

* * * *

June 21st

I'm sitting in the corner at a church gathering where about fifty people have met to pray for the future of our congregation.

Most people have their eyes closed, but I can't concentrate and start scanning the room. There's definitely something going on in here. The elder next to me would no doubt say the Holy Spirit is at work. People look relaxed, serene almost. Apart from one man. His face is contorted and he looks as if he's in real pain. He keeps nodding his head, whispering, 'Yes, Lord, yes, Lord.'

I'm blatantly gawping, but out of the corner of my eye I see a slight movement and realize that someone is staring at *me*. It's the elder, and our eyes meet for a second before she closes hers again. There's no reaction apart from a strange twitching movement around the corners of her mouth. My cheeks start to burn. Why do I always feel such a fraud at these events? It seems that the longer I'm a Christian the more bemused I become. Even when I sense that the Holy Spirit is around, I can never quite pin down what it all means, what might be going on. And I still don't know what to make of the various reports of healings and miracles that I hear about in the Christian circles I move in.

Then there's all the other stuff that goes on, the endless debates that Christians seem to embroil themselves in.

Over the last few months, I've listened to discussions on women and leadership, homosexuality, heaven and hell, and whether it matters if you don't believe in a literal virgin birth, or a literal resurrection.

Then there's the latest hot potato – Christian leaders putting their foot in it left, right and centre; and, of course, everyone blames the wicked media for taking their words out of context.

As someone who was part of that evil empire until fairly recently, I do get quite defensive. Can't we just take responsibility for own words and how they might be interpreted?

When all the talk is over, when the debates have run their course, I sometimes wonder what being a Christian is all about. There are so many different shades of opinion out there, so many very clever and learned people claiming so many different things about the faith that I still do believe has changed my life. It should be very simple, but it's so easy to get distracted.

Now we're splitting into small groups to talk and pray. The elder next to me turns and smiles, then invites a teenager who is playing with the zip on his coat to join us. We chat for a while about the months ahead, and what they might hold for us as a church. The boy starts. At first he stammers, but once he finds his feet he's off. He talks with a passion about winning people for Christ, about helping the poor and lonely.

I close my eyes and pray that some of his enthusiasm would rub off on me, and that I'll finally learn not to make my faith so complicated. And soon I do feel more peaceful. Prayer is good. Prayer is the one thing I can do and not question every five minutes. I believe in prayer.

Soon it's time for Holy Communion, and we stay in our groups. At our church it's the custom for us to tear off a bit of bread and dunk it in the wine, and that's what I do.

The boy's been deep in thought, though. He eats his bread, then takes a big glug straight from the cup. Almost straight away his face drops as he looks at the next table and realizes he might have done something wrong. But the elder doesn't miss a beat. As if it were entirely normal, she takes her bread, then she too puts the cup to her mouth and takes a sip.

I look at her. I was just asking what my faith was all about and I think I've been given a pretty big hint.

The Lord has just shown me a simple act of kindness and acceptance. And suddenly he seems very near.

* * * *

Wednesday, 8 p.m.

Dear Dad,
The police rang me yesterday. It's all right, I'm not about to be arrested. It did shake me up, though, and got me thinking about my past again.

The detective was very polite and used my maiden name. It turns out they'd found my mobile number in the files of a journalist who'd been arrested, and thought my phone might have been hacked.

I had to smile. I explained I used to work for the newspaper at the centre of the investigation; in fact, I'd sat opposite the reporter for five years, so he had my number for legiti-mate reasons.

Afterwards, I walked round the garden and thought about my former colleague, and I prayed for him. What must it be like to have the spotlight of the world's media on you and your family, everyone wondering how you could have done what you did?

I'm not judging him, though. It could so easily have been me.

I shut my eyes then, and pictured myself in the tabloid newsroom, joking with my colleagues; young, full of bravado. We thought we were the masters of the universe.

Now here I am in a very different situation. And all through God's grace.

It's very easy to 'demonize' someone who's done something particularly awful, and of course, justice is important. But there seem to be certain categories of 'sinner' that Christians have decided to pick out for special treatment.

It's almost as if they'd have to 'prove' their repentance before being 'allowed' in.

Does that have anything to do with grace, Dad?

And I'm not just talking about conservative evangelicals who seem obsessed with homosexuality and moral failings. I reckon there could be 'guardians of acceptance' in the so-called 'liberal' wing too. To be welcomed into their church, do you need to have the 'right' ethics or politics? How can you be a Christian if you read, or even write for, the 'wrong' newspaper?

Perhaps I'm being unfair, but sometimes I just can't be bothered with it all, Dad. I am trying to follow Jesus as best I can. Must I start to police the salvation of others? Is it any of my business what goes on in people's hearts? It's between them and God, surely?

Friday, 2 p.m.

I thought I saw you in the park this morning. Just for a split second; it must have been a trick of the light.

I was meeting Val, but had arrived early. Lucy was asleep in her buggy, and Daniel had found a good stick to play with.

We walked up to the willow tree where you used to take Neil and me when we were small. I remember you telling us that willows take root very easily, that often new trees will grow from twigs or broken branches that have fallen to the ground. I thought that was very odd indeed. I mean if things are broken, how can something new come from them?

I've been thinking a lot about dramatic 'fast-track' healing recently, and how God seems to work differently with me. My journey has been all about time, nothing instant – seeds sown in my heart, sometimes many years before. A tree growing very slowly, perhaps.

And I think I might even be learning to listen, and recognize God's direction in my life. Sometimes it starts as a gentle niggle in the back of my mind, but gets stronger and stronger, and I don't get any peace until I've prayed or done something about it.

I've got a long way to go, though. I still struggle with worry and 'letting go', and all the other strange and worrying things I've come across in church.

And yet, and yet . . . when I'm just about to give up, I hear the gentle, encouraging voices of Christians I've encountered in the last few years.

I stood under the tree and pictured Uncle Dave – 'Jesus Christ is the key to interpretation of the Scriptures, just hold on to that.' Jenny from cell group – 'Pray, just pray!' And our pastor – 'Keep running, keep going, do it for God, do it for him.'

At that moment, Daniel yelled, 'Auntie Val!' and we headed off towards her. But something stopped me and I turned to look back at the willow tree. It was then that I thought I saw you; you were holding the hand of a little girl and looking down at her with a smile on your face.

Your loving daughter,
Ruth

* * * *

July 1st

Val's been waiting for us in the park, and when we finally reach her she seems rather flushed, and it looks like she's been crying.

'Are you OK?' I ask. 'Is everything all right with your mum?'

She just nods and we walk for a while. When we reach a small clearing in the trees, Val stops and turns to me. 'So what happens at your church when people "go to the front"? Tell me about the weird stuff. No holds barred.'

I study her. She seems serious, but you can never be sure. 'Well, you just talk to them for a little while,' I say, 'and then – well, it's not that strange, but at the church I go to you put your hand on their shoulder, I don't know why, and you pray for them. It's quite simple, really.'

'OK, then,' Val almost whispers. I nearly make a joke, but something stops me.

'Val, would you like me to pray for you? Is that what you're saying?'

'Yes, please.'

'Now?' She nods again, and then says simply, 'For a baby.'

Tears threaten, but I swallow hard and check on the children. Lucy's still asleep and Daniel is digging close by.

'Can I?'

'Yes,' she says, and I place my hand carefully on her shoulder. It's a warm, sunny morning. I look round the clearing and it seems to me as if rays of light are dancing through the branches.

Val closes her eyes, and I pray.

* * * *

July 28th

It's our daughter's dedication and we're in church, surrounded by family and friends.

Not all of them are entirely happy to be here, though, and I look round to check everyone's OK. Neil is at the end of the row and Val's right behind me. I wonder what they're thinking right now.

It's getting more and more difficult for me to remember how I felt when I walked in here the first few times.

The problem is that this all now seems, well, normal to me – as normal as it will ever get, I guess.

Surely my brother and my friend must have seen how everything's changed since I started going to church.

Val still thinks the difference has little to do with spiritual things; more that my husband came into my life and gave me the stability I needed. But I know that he and my children were a gift from God – and I'm never going to forget that. I'm never going to stop thanking him. Sometimes I worry that something awful will happen to one of them, and I don't know how I would cope. Even now, sitting here in church, I should feel safe, but I know from all the news stories that I've written that lives can be devastated in an instant. Accidents happen and illnesses strike. Is the curse of really loving someone the knowledge that you could lose them? Any illusion we have of control is just that.

Oh dear. This isn't good. We're due at the front after the next song, and I'm trying to fight back tears.

Val taps me on the shoulder. 'Are you all right?' I look round. 'Yes, just getting a bit emotional. I'll be OK in a minute.'

She doesn't look convinced. I sit down, and as I start to flick through my Bible in search of a calming passage, a piece of paper flutters out on to the floor.

Val picks it up and reads it, first to herself and then, quietly, in my ear.

'"God is ultimately in control. God is there, whether I feel him or not. God has a plan for my life, whether I understand it or not. God works in the way he chooses (the best way), whether I like it or not."' She pauses for a second, then hisses, 'Where did you get this?'

'A friend heard it at a conference she went to, and wrote it out for me.'

'And do you believe it?'

'Yes, I do.'

'Well, then. Get a grip.' My friend squeezes my hand.

The band strikes up. It's a pacey version of 'Be Thou My Vision'.

Val looks excited. 'I really like this one,' she says.

I smile. So do I. And I watch in amazement as she starts to sing, 'I ever with Thee, Thou with me, Lord . . .'[2]

Further along the row Neil catches my eye and grins. He's joining in too. 'Thou my soul's Shelter, Thou my high Tower . . .'

What's going on? Is something finally happening here? Is it too much to hope that this might just be the start of them finding a space that fits, something that makes sense to them inside church?

The way I have . . . I look around at my husband, my children, my friends and church family. I am so grateful to be where I am, where sometimes God feels close, and sometimes he doesn't, but where I'm never far from people who inspire me, who give me strength – and show me Jesus.

So I close my eyes and lift my voice, 'Heart of my own heart, whatever befall, Still be my Vision, O Ruler of all.'

* * * *

Dear Dad,

I'm standing in the Garden of Remembrance. Daniel is racing around in the late afternoon sunshine, pretending to be a train. Lucy is sitting in her buggy, laughing and clapping her hands together.

Your rose bush looks lovely, and the words on your plaque are faded, but I can still just about read them: 'Beloved husband, father, brother, friend. Forever loved and missed.'

I can't tell you how much I miss you still, and how every milestone that passes is tinged with sadness because you're not here to see them.

I hope you'd be proud of me now, of me as an adult, of what's happened in my life.

I was so proud of you. Sometimes, when I'm in a situation and I feel unsure, I imagine you walking beside me, and it gives me strength.

Perhaps some Christians think I should be imagining Jesus instead, but if I want to feel cherished and secure, I think of the people in my life who have made me feel that way. And then I thank God for putting them there. Perhaps that means I still have a long way to go.

Funnily enough, in spite of everything I've agonized over, I do feel peaceful now.

I read recently that the greatest challenge facing Christians at this time is how we read the Bible, and that struck a chord.

Can I take wisdom and instruction from the Old Testament, while ignoring the God who wipes out families on a whim?

Do I have to take a stance on every issue, and have scripture to back it up? And when my children ask me exactly what I believe, will it be OK to say I just don't know? Will it be enough to tell them that God is on our side and he is good? But what about hell, Dad? What about the people who say 'It's not for me'?

On Sunday, our pastor was preaching about judgement, but not in the way you might imagine. He told us he's actually been asked to make clear at funerals of unbelievers that as they'd rejected Christ they would not be in heaven.

Everyone looked shocked, but I wasn't.

I'm not going to dwell on what some Christians told Neil and I after you died. I prefer to remember the kind woman who put her hands on my shoulders and told me you would still know us – at every stage in our lives.

I pray that's true. I pray that because you knew love, you knew Jesus after all.

Thank you for being such an amazing dad. Thank you for making it easy for me to see God as a good father.
I'll let you know how I get on, but until then I remain, ever,
Your loving daughter,
Ruth

AN INTERVIEW WITH THE AUTHOR

Ruth Dickinson, editor of *Christianity* magazine, which first published Ruth Roberts's column, interviews her about her experiences of becoming a Christian, and how she found those early days of church . . .

[RD] How would you characterize your journey to faith overall?

There is a slight tendency to idealize becoming a Christian as someone who goes along to a meeting, hears the gospel and puts their hand up, then responds and goes to the front and becomes a Christian.

Then, slowly but surely, they are assimilated into the church. They become like everybody else in the church and they believe all the right things.

[RD] You mean, this idea of having one powerful encounter with Jesus and then they are a believer . . .

Absolutely, I went on an Alpha course, which is part of the story, and you read in the Alpha newsletters about these people who have these powerful experiences and then they change. Sometimes it is a slow journey but from that point onwards they change as long as they keep on going to church and doing the right things. Well I think with me it was very long and drawn out. For me it started when I was working for *The News of the World* in the 1990s and my life was a bit of a mess to put it mildly.

[RD] What happened?

I tried to clear up my life, I was drinking too much, I was smoking too much (not that smoking is a terrible thing, but it probably wasn't very good for me), my personal life was a mess.

People know about *The News of the World* now because of what has happened in the past couple of years, but it really wasn't a very nice place to work and I did want to get out and I did want to change, I wanted to be a different person. I just didn't really know what to do, I did try and look at other religions and I did try to stop drinking and sort stuff out.

It just didn't work. I found myself walking into this Orthodox church in Poland.

[RD] What were you doing in Poland?

I was on holiday with a friend. It was a walking holiday seeing the sights. I was dreading going back to work and walking around with this horrible feeling in my stomach.

166

I don't think that I was depressed but I felt wretched. I walked into this church, there was nothing evangelical about it, it was just priests lighting candles, incense and I simply knelt down and said 'help'.

[RD] Before that point, had you tried consciously to seek God?

I did go to a youth group in my teens, but I didn't take it very seriously, I went for the social aspect more than anything. It was a very conservative youth group, but I think the seeds were sown there. That was always the God that I cried out to.

I have always believed in God and I did pray for people when I was working as a journalist when I would come across horrible situations.

[RD] So there had always been awareness about a belief in God?

I had always believed in God but I just didn't like Christians very much. I didn't like the anti-woman, the anti-gay, the very rigid, or at least my perception of, the moral code. My perception was that Christians were judgemental hypocrites or woolly do-gooders and a bit pathetic.

[RD] So what was it that happened in Poland in that church with the candles lit when you cried out to God?

I just started crying. Crying is a common theme in my testimony, I just felt that everything was wrong, I felt awful and unhappy.

I did have a bit of a problem with drink. I had reached that stage where . . . I have a very vivid memory of waking up with a hangover from hell, I woke up and I couldn't remember how I got home and couldn't remember much of the evening and I ran to my handbag and started tossing everything out and looking for receipts to try and piece together where I'd been because I couldn't remember.

I was a Bridget Jones gone horribly wrong: I would sit at home and drink a bottle of wine alone and then wake up in the morning worried that I had phoned someone while drunk. That was obviously a big thing that took a long time to be sorted. Unlike some of the testimonies I've read I didn't suddenly stop having that desire to smoke or drink when I came to faith.

[RD] Would you say the moment in Poland was the key moment of you committing yourself?

It was a big moment because things did happen after that, I got a new job, I started to feel more 'peaceful' about things. But it was a few years before I occasionally turned up at a church my friends went to. I'd just stand at the back and run away as quickly as I could when it was over. A few years after that I asked my husband (he was my boyfriend at the time), if he would come to church with me, and he agreed.

[RD] Was he resistant at all?

I think he was because although he was a 'lapsed' Christian I think he was worried that this particular church was going to be a bit wacky. It was me that literally dragged him back really.

[RD] Even though you weren't sure yourself?

I wanted to go to church and I realized that I needed church, I wanted some form of spirituality in my life.

The only message that I got from that church was grace, total grace. That was really attractive to me, I don't think that I was really aware of what was going on but it was grace. Even to the extent that the pastor came up to my husband and me and said 'Well I don't think I have seen you before . . .' and he was just such a charming man.

We said that we were getting married soon, and that we weren't getting married in a church and he didn't even bat an eyelid, we just started talking about our honeymoon in Italy. There was no judgement, you felt totally accepted as how you were.

Then we signed up to the Alpha course, and that was lovely, the people were fun, it was interesting and we had these great debates and that was when I made the commitment.

[RD] What happened over the course?

It was like there was this battle going on in my head. I got quite emotional and obsessive about this. Do I go for this or should it be something that I dip in and out off, that sort of thing. And I remember making the proper commitment.

At work during lunch I remember going for a walk and thinking I would have to be like a child and trust, and out of nowhere a group of school children appeared . . .

To me it felt very strongly that God was talking to me and that God was there. I went for a run on Valentine's Day and I did actually say, right, that's it.

[RD] How was going back to work as a Christian?

It was fine really, and I didn't really care. They were lovely people, they teased me a little bit. I was still me, I remember completely losing it one day and standing up shouting, and one person shouted to everyone in the newsroom, 'the Christian is swearing!'

I used to try and get people to go on Alpha courses. There was one woman in particular that I suggested went on an Alpha course, I don't know if she did, she talked about going to HTB [Holy Trinity, Brompton] and checking it out.

One of my colleagues who is gay, said: 'How can you go to a church?' I still get upset when I think about it. I didn't change towards him, but he was confused about what I believed. I think he was worried that I wouldn't want to be his friend any more.

[RD] Have you got any reflections on the Church in general? About how evangelical Christians present themselves in public life, in the real world . . .

I do think that perception is really important. I think we are in danger of misrepresenting Jesus. I think if the Church is seen as a place of judgement and condemnation, rather than a place of compassion and safety, then people are not going to want to come through the doors.

I think that the church does need to engage in a better way with the media.

[RD] What do you mean by engaging in a better way?

Ordinary people who just go about their business see the Anglican Church to be what is happening in the Church, full stop. They don't know the nuances, so they see issues about splits, gay people, women, the arguing with each other . . .

What I would like to see in the media is more of the counter-cultural stories, stories that show us reflecting who Jesus really is. Stories like the woman who donated her kidney to a stranger she met at a party because she is a Christian, or people who have managed to forgive.

[RD] Is there anything you would like to say about the pressure for new Christians to conform to church life?

I didn't feel a lot of pressure, but there is an expectation to conform. I don't want to criticize the church that I was at, but as a general observation I don't think that there is a special formula that you go to church, you hear the gospel, and you convert, I don't think it is necessarily like that.

[RD] How was your integration in to the church post-Alpha? How was your journey into Christendom?

It was a journey into weirdness to a certain degree. It was all the stuff like people closing their eyes and throwing their hands in the air and I was thinking 'flip, that's odd, I don't think I will ever be like that', yet being so fascinated by it, the people were so kind and full of grace.

For me the more challenging aspect was realizing I'd come into this institution, where my experiences and my beliefs probably were somewhat at odds with what I thought at the time most Christians believed.

[RD] What are you talking about here . . . ?

I am talking about the gay issue and the way women are treated. I was quite staggered when I found out that there are churches that don't have women as leaders. Then there is the gay issue . . .

[RD] What do you mean by the gay issue?

That homosexuality is wrong, and I had gay friends in the industry where I worked. I couldn't imagine telling people that who they are is wrong and I still struggle with that. I have found out since that there are different ways of talking about or looking at that issue.

[RD] What else did you struggle with in Christian culture?

Well from us being in an evangelical, charismatic church it was the laying on of hands, praying for people, going to the front to be prayed for was a big thing for me for a long time.

A challenge for me is the surrendering thing, of giving over your worries, and so for me going up to the front and making myself vulnerable enough to let someone pray for me, or put their hand on my shoulder, was a massive thing that took quite a while to become comfortable with in that sort of culture.

[RD] Why do you think that you were uncomfortable in that sort of culture? Do you think that it is a personal thing? Or is it more to do with what is going on in the church and it being a bit weird.

It is weird to outsiders. When I first started some of my friends clearly thought that I had been sucked into some sort of cult. I remember trying to explain the raising of hands thing to them, trying to equate it with football matches and music

173

festivals but they weren't convinced. I think most people who don't have a church background would be wary of 'going to the front' on a Sunday morning to close your eyes and share your worries in front of people you've never met before. But I'm not sure that's what stops people coming through our doors, I worry that people feel church is out of touch, and more importantly that they're going to be judged. In my experience that couldn't have been further from the truth.

NOTES

PART TWO: HOPES AND FEARS

[1] 1 Peter 5:8
[2] Mark 16:8, KJV
[3] Mark 16:17,18

PART THREE: HOLD TIGHT

[1] Revelation 21:4
[2] John 14:6

PART FOUR: MAKING MUSIC

[1] Mark 9:24
[2] Mark 2:17
[3] Isaiah 43:1

PART FIVE: LITTLE CHILDREN

[1] 'How Great is Our God' written by Ed Cash, Jesse Reeves and Chris Tomlin copyright © 2004 worshiptogether.com Songs/ sixsteps Music/ASCAP (adm. by EMI CMG Publishing)/ Alletrop Music/BMI All rights reserved. Used by permission. Alletrop Music/Music Services (Admin. by Song Solutions CopyCare www.songsolutions.org).

PART SIX: THE LORD REIGNS

[1] Matt Redman, 'The Father's Song', The Father's Song, 2000.
[2] Dallán Forgaill (*ca*. 530–598) translated by Mary E. Byrne, 1880–1931 and versified by Eleanor Henrietta Hull, 1860-1935.